D0947496

Sainte, final page of the holograph, signed by Ravel and dated December 1896. (The key signature is four flats.)

MAURICE RAVEL

SONGS

1896-1914

Edited by Arbie Orenstein

DOVER PUBLICATIONS, INC., NEW YORK

Deux Mélodies hébraïques © 1915 Durand S.A. Éditions Musicales
Éditions A.R.I.M.A. and Durand S.A. Éditions Musicales
Joint Publication
Reprinted By Permission Of The Publisher
Sole Representative U.S.A., Theodore Presser Company

This Dover edition, first published in 1990,
is a new collection of thirteen works, originally published as follows:
Sainte, Durand & Cie, 1907.
Épigrammes de Clément Marot, E. Demets, 1900.
Manteau de fleurs, J. Hamelle, 1906.
Shéhérazade, Durand & Cie, 1911.
Cinq Mélodies populaires grecques, Durand & Cie, 1906.
Noël des jouets, Bellon Ponscarme, n.d.
Histoires naturelles, Durand & Cie, 1907.
Vocalise-Étude en forme de Habanera, Alphonse Leduc, 1909.
Les Grands Vents venus d'outremer, Durand & Cie, 1907.
Sur l'herbe, Durand & Cie, 1907.
Chants populaires, P. Jurgenson, 1911.
Trois Poèmes de Stéphane Mallarmé, Durand & Cie, 1914.
Deux Mélodies hébraïques, Durand & Cie, 1915.

We are grateful to the Music Library of Queens College
for the loan of some of the scores for reproduction.

Manufactured in the United States of America
Dover Publications, Inc.
31 East 2nd Street
Mineola, N.Y. 11501

Library of Congress Cataloging-in-Publication Data

Ravel, Maurice, 1875–1937.
[Songs. Selections]
Songs, 1896–1914.

French and English words; French words with English
translations also printed as texts.
1. Songs with piano.   I. Orenstein, Arbie.   II. Title.
M1620.R2507   1990   90-750799
ISBN 0-486-26354-1

Contents

Preface

This collection of songs by Maurice Ravel (1875–1937) contains most of his music in this genre written up to 1914.[1] Only a few songs were completed in the postwar years: *Ronsard à son âme* (1924), the *Chansons madécasses* (1925–26), *Rêves* (1927), and *Don Quichotte à Dulcinée* (1932–33). Thus, Ravel's contribution to the *mélodie* was small in quantity but distinguished in quality. The first editions of the songs, mostly published by Durand, were carefully done, and only two minor corrections have been made.

Arbie Orenstein
The Aaron Copland School of Music
Queens College

---

[1] The following songs, which do not appear in this volume, were edited by the present writer and published separately by Salabert in 1975: *Ballade de la reine morte d'aimer* (c. 1893, poem by Roland de Marès), *Un Grand Sommeil noir* (1895, poem by Paul Verlaine), *Chanson du rouet* (1898, poem by Leconte de Lisle), *Si morne!* (1898, poem by Émile Verhaeren), *Tripatos* (1909, a Greek folk song), and the *Chanson écossaise* (1910, poem by Robert Burns).

Introduction

Maurice Ravel's legacy consists of some sixty compositions written between the early 1890s and the 1930s. Slightly more than half of these works are instrumental: fifteen pieces and suites for the piano, eight chamber works, six orchestral works, several ballets, and two piano concerti. The vocal music consists of eighteen songs and song cycles with accompaniment for piano, chamber ensemble, or orchestra; several settings of folk melodies; one work for unaccompanied mixed chorus; and two operas. It would be misleading to divide this music into periods of apprenticeship and maturity, for Ravel's earliest compositions were on the whole remarkably characteristic. The "Habanera" and the *Menuet antique* were written by a twenty-year-old student, and with the completion of *Jeux d'eau* at the age of twenty-six the composer's style was firmly set. These early works indicate many of the trends he would pursue: a predilection for dance rhythms, the music of Spain, archaic pastiche, and contemporary impressionistic techniques. Thus, from the outset, Ravel's approach to composition might be called metamorphic—that is, in each new undertaking he would cover fresh ground, placing his personal stamp upon widely differing techniques and idioms. This is particularly evident in the vocal music. From the preciosity of Clément Marot to the complex symbolism of Stéphane Mallarmé, from Renaissance Alexandrines to modern poems in prose, Ravel rarely repeated himself. Most often, he turned to free verse *(vers libres)* and prose poems. He believed that setting a text implied creating a new work of art and that the musician thereby became an equal partner with the author. Thus, a text could be modified, as long as its general sense and poetic beauty were in no way jeopardized. The spiritual sources of Ravel's vocal art range from the composers of the French Renaissance chanson to the work of Massenet, Mussorgsky, Chabrier, Satie, Fauré, and Debussy. The peripheral influence of Wagner and Schoenberg may also be observed. Unlike the more adventurous instrumental style, the vocal writing employs traditional tessitura with practically no attempt at virtuosity. Depending on the song, one may observe a lyrical vocal line that extends over a limited range *(Sainte)*, quasi-parlando writing *(Histoires naturelles)*, or some instrumental angularity *(Trois Poèmes de Stéphane Mallarmé)*. The accompaniment will occasionally establish a uniform atmosphere, deriving from the general mood of the poem *(Épigrammes de Clément Marot)*, while at other times the text may be interpreted quite literally *(Histoires naturelles)*. Ineluctably attracted to exoticism, Ravel willingly harmonized folk melodies from many nations. He preferred having the melodies sung in their original language, and performed, if possible, with orchestral accompaniment. An interpreter would thus have to cope with some ten languages.

A complete accounting of the elements in Ravel's art would run a gamut from Gregorian chant to Gershwin, passing through the Renaissance, Baroque, Classical, and Romantic eras. He managed to keep his personal touch in a style that varied from the classical simplicity of *Ma Mère l'Oye* to the transcendental romantic virtuosity of *Gaspard de la nuit*, from the luxuriant, caressing sonority of *Daphnis et Chloé* to the austere violence of the *Chansons madécasses*, and from Renaissance pastiche to adaptations of jazz. His achievement is not eclectic, nor can it be summed up in one all-encompassing label. It is thoroughly French in orientation, and is solidly based upon traditional practice. In the last analysis, like any other significant artist, Ravel fashioned his own laws and created his own universe.

Notes on the Music[1]

SAINTE (Saint; poem by Stéphane Mallarmé; composed 1896; dedicated to Madame Edmond Bonniot, née Mallarmé; first performance: Hélène Luquiens and Ravel, June 8, 1907, Paris)

In December 1865, Mallarmé (1842–1898) wrote to the poet Théodore Aubanel, describing *Sainte* as a "short melodic poem." The poem's original title was "Sainte Cécile jouant sur l'aile d'un chérubin" ("Saint Cecilia Playing on the Wing of a Cherub"), and Ravel's setting captures the contemplative mood by means of a quasi-liturgical vocal line accompanied by slow-moving chords. The many unresolved chords of the seventh and ninth point to the pathbreaking influence of Ravel's colleague and mentor Erik Satie. (Ravel modified three words in Mallarmé's poem: ". . . De *la* viole étincelant/Jadis *selon* flûte ou mandore; . . . Jadis selon vêpre *ou* complie.")

ÉPIGRAMMES DE CLÉMENT MAROT (Epigrams by Clément Marot)
I. D'Anne qui me jecta de la neige (On Anne throwing snow at me).
II. D'Anne jouant de l'espinette (On Anne playing the spinet).
(I. 1899; II. 1896; dedicated to M. Hardy-Thé; first performance: M. Hardy-Thé and Ravel, January 27, 1900, Paris)

The art of Clément Marot (1496–1544) has qualities that appeal to most Frenchmen: delicate charm, polish, clarity, and wit. Ravel was particularly attracted to the orthographical curiosities of Renaissance French. The poet's original titles, "D'Anne qui luy jecta de la neige" and "D'Anne," appear to have been modified by the composer. The songs exhibit gentle refinement and preciosity, coupled with a deliberately archaic use of parallel fifths and octaves.

---

[1]I wish to thank Columbia University Press for permission to quote from my book *Ravel: Man and Musician* (1975).

MANTEAU DE FLEURS (Mantle of Flowers; poem by Paul Gravollet; 1903).

Paul Gravollet (the stage name of Paul Barthélémy Jeulin, 1863–1936) performed secondary roles at the Comédie Française and also wrote plays and collections of poetry. His poems have remained obscure with good reason, and "Manteau de fleurs" proved to be a rare lapse in Ravel's fastidious selection of texts for musical adaptation. Gravollet sent his poems to the leading French composers of the day, and managed to convince twenty-two of them to set his work. The result was an undistinguished collection of songs entitled *Les Frissons*. With its numerous measured thirty-second notes, the piano accompaniment often suggests orchestral sonorities. Ravel's orchestration of the accompaniment (still unpublished) is somewhat better, but, like Debussy in *Dans le jardin*, he was unable to overcome Gravollet's banal poetry. Ravel later returned to the motif of flowers in his ballet libretto *Adélaïde, ou le langage des fleurs*, based on the *Valses nobles et sentimentales*.

SHÉHÉRAZADE (Scheherazade)
I. Asie (Asia); dedicated to Mademoiselle Jeane [*sic*] Hatto.
II. La Flûte enchantée (The Magic Flute); dedicated to Madame René de Saint-Marceaux.
III. L'Indifférent (The Unresponsive One); dedicated to Madame Sigismond Bardac.
(Poems by Tristan Klingsor; 1903; first performance: Jane Hatto, Alfred Cortot conducting, May 17, 1904, Paris)

In his poems Tristan Klingsor (the pseudonym of Arthur Justin Léon Leclère, 1874–1966, French poet, painter, art critic, and composer) strove for clarity, balance, and, above all, communication with the reader:

My poems are like sketches. . . . A poem should be that already; a point of departure for a song, or a melody. . . . Perhaps that is why I have had the good fortune to please musicians. You see, I attempted not to be merely a rhymer, I attempted to be a rhythmist. Rhythm, in poetry, music, and in painting, is the artist's foremost resource.[1]

In discussing the *fin de siècle* in France, Tristan Klingsor observed that "the Orient was in the air, through Bakst, Rimsky-Korsakov, and Doctor Mardrus, who translated the *Thousand and One Nights*." In 1903, Klingsor completed a collection of one hundred poems entitled *Shéhérazade*. The title was taken from Rimsky-Korsakov's orchestral suite, and the collection centers about the Orient and its kaleidoscopic lure. Born just one year apart, Ravel and Klingsor had spent many evenings together discussing music and poetry with colleagues, and at the composer's request the poet declaimed "Asie," "La Flûte enchantée," and "L'Indifférent" for him. Thereupon, Ravel went into his customary isolation when composing, reappearing to request some minor changes in the text of "Asie," to which the poet agreed.[2] Ravel was attracted not only to the oriental lure of Klingsor's collection, but also to its subtle free verse and its vivid pictorial imagery. The text is set syllabically, often in a quasi-recitative fashion, underpinned by orchestral motifs. This apparently accounts for the composer's acknowledgment of Debussy's "spiritual influence" on the song cycle; the vocal line in *Pelléas et Mélisande*, however, is generally closer to recitative.

In adapting Klingsor's poems, Ravel was primarily concerned with transforming the rhythmic subtleties of free verse into melody, a direction he would pursue in the *Histoires naturelles* and in his first opera, *L'Heure espagnole*. *Shéhérazade* gradually decreases in intensity, from the rich voluptuousness of "Asie" through the gentle lyricism of "La Flûte enchantée" to the languid sensuousness of "L'Indifférent." Subtitled "Three poems for voice and orchestra," this haunting triptych was Ravel's second artistic encounter with oriental fantasy, the first being his Overture to *Shéhérazade* (1898, first published by Salabert in 1975). If the songs are performed with piano, the pianist must try to capture the variegated colors of the orchestral version.

---

[1]L. J. Pronger, *La Poésie de Tristan Klingsor* (Paris: M. J. Minard, 1965), p. 65.

[2]Ravel was upset that his interpreter, soprano Jane Hatto, would have to sing about a pipe ("Like Sinbad placing my old Arabic pipe between my lips from time to time"), and he suggested that the pipe be replaced by a cup ("Like Sinbad raising my old Arabic cup to my lips from time to time").

CINQ MÉLODIES POPULAIRES GRECQUES (Five Greek Folk Songs)
  I.   Chanson de la mariée (Bride's Song).
  II. Là-bas, vers l'église (Yonder by the Church).
  III. Quel Galant m'est comparable (What Gallant Can Be Compared with Me?).
  IV. Chanson des cueilleuses de lentisques (Song of the Girls Collecting Mastic).
  V.   Tout gai! (Be Gay!).
       (Melodies and texts collected by Pericles Matsa and Hubert Pernot; 1904–6; first performance of the complete cycle: Marguerite Babaïan, at a lecture-recital presented by M. D. Calvocoressi in Paris during the 1905–6 season)

The genesis of the *Cinq Mélodies populaires grecques* may be traced to a lecture that the French musicologist Pierre Aubry planned to give on the songs of oppressed peoples (Greeks and Armenians). He asked the critic Michel D. Calvocoressi to select some Greek songs for illustrative purposes, and after making his choice, Calvocoressi taught them phonetically to the singer Louise Thomasset, who agreed to perform them on short notice but wished to have piano accompaniments for the melodies. The critic thereupon turned to Ravel, who wrote accompaniments to five melodies within some thirty-six hours, thus marking his first venture into the realm of folklore. Of the five songs performed by Mlle Thomasset, only two (nos. 3 and 4) were later incorporated into the *Cinq Mélodies populaires grecques*; the others remained unpublished, as Ravel found their accompaniments "too brief." As a result, three other melodies were later set, and since Ravel admired Marguerite Babaïan's interpretations of them, he subsequently set a sixth Greek melody for her, *Tripatos*. Ravel's accompaniments blend perfectly with their respective melodies, skillfully capturing the various folk expressions of love, faith, and joy.

NOËL DES JOUETS (The Toys' Christmas; poem by Maurice Ravel; 1905; dedicated to Madame Jean Cruppi; first performance: Jane Bathori and Ravel, March 24, 1906, Paris; Jane Bathori, Ravel conducting, April 26, 1906, Paris)

This song reveals Ravel's modest ability as a poet, and the depiction of a Christmas manger, with toy animals, flocks, and angels, affirms his fascination with the pristine world of childhood. The clarity and tenderness of the poem are not unrelated to some of Jules Renard's *Histoires naturelles*, and passages in the piano recall the second movement of Ravel's Sonatine (1903–5). He observed that the music is "clear and plain, like the mechanical toys of the poem," and the parallel seconds and concluding fanfare in the accompaniment will reappear with increased effect in *Ma Mère l'Oye*.

HISTOIRES NATURELLES (Natural Histories)
  I.   Le Paon (The Peacock); dedicated to Madame Jane Bathori.
  II. Le Grillon (The Cricket); dedicated to Mademoiselle Madeleine Picard.
  III. Le Cygne (The Swan); dedicated to Madame Alfred Edwards, née Godebska.
  IV. Le Martin-Pêcheur (The Kingfisher); dedicated to Émile Engel.
  V.   La Pintade (The Guinea Fowl); dedicated to Roger Ducasse.
       (Poems by Jules Renard; 1906; first performance: Jane Bathori and Ravel, January 12, 1907, Paris.)

In September 1895, shortly before the publication of the *Histoires naturelles*, Jules Renard (1864–1910) wrote in his *Journal*: "*Histoires naturelles*—Buffon[1] described animals in order to give pleasure to men. As for me, I would wish to be pleasing to the animals themselves. If they were able to read my miniature *Histoires naturelles*, I should wish that it would make them smile." The subtlety of Renard's technique has been perceptively analyzed as follows:

Intimately bound with the overall sentence structure is the skillful interlocking of linguistic levels. Rhetoric and colloquialism are juxtaposed; the polished literary phrase is preceded or followed by a matter-of-fact aside. This variation enables Renard to change his point of view, moving into and out of the mind of his subject at will (and in this respect at least he is indebted to La Fontaine). In this way he is able to achieve changes of tempo and subtle effects of irony.[2]

Two important spiritual ancestors of Ravel's song cycle were Chabrier's charming and humorous animal songs and Mussorgsky's incomplete opera *The Marriage*. In setting Gogol's play, Mussorgsky observed that he was "crossing the Rubicon. This is living prose in music . . . this is reverence toward the language of humanity, this is a reproduction of simple human speech."[3] Mussorgsky's goal was adopted by Ravel, who observed that in the *Histoires naturelles* "the diction must lead the music." Jane Bathori recalled that in the *Histoires naturelles* Ravel

> had completely broken with what is customarily called "melody." The voice was subservient to the prosody, which embraced the text to such an extent that the mute *e*'s were no longer heard. This procedure, which Ravel also used in *L'Heure espagnole*, disconcerted quite a few singers, but made them acquire a more supple and more animated diction.[4]

In order to approximate the tone of conversation, the meter is frequently changed, and the melody often moves within a limited range. In this regard, the critic Émile Vuillermoz made the following personal observation:

> When Ravel made one of those razor-edged remarks of which he alone possessed the secret, he used to make a characteristic gesture: he put his right hand quickly behind his back, described a sort of ironical pirouette, cast down his mischievously sparkling eyes and let his voice suddenly drop a fourth or a fifth. In the *Histoires naturelles* and *L'Heure espagnole* one finds this characteristic intonation in all sorts of places. It is Ravel's own voice, his pronunciation, his well-known mannerisms that have produced this *quasi parlando* melody.[5]

Above all, the *Histoires naturelles* reaffirm the marked sensitivity of author and composer in depicting the magical world of animal life.

Renard's seventy sketches of animal life were illustrated by Félix Vallotton (1896), Henri de Toulouse-Lautrec (1899), and Pierre Bonnard (1904). Moreover, Lucien Guitry and other leading actors of the day declaimed the poems in public. Although viewed with suspicion and hostility in 1907, Ravel's interpretation of the *Histoires naturelles* has been vindicated by time, and the cycle now appears to be an important and original contribution to French song.

---

[1]Renard's title is indebted to the noted eighteenth-century French naturalist Georges-Louis Leclerc, Comte de Buffon, whose monumental *Histoire naturelle* was published in forty-four volumes between 1749 and 1804.

[2]Basil Deane, "Renard, Ravel, and the 'Histoires naturelles,'" *Australian Journal of French Studies* 1 (1964), p. 179.

[3]J. Leyda and S. Bertensson, *The Mussorgsky Reader* (New York: W. W. Norton, 1947), p. 112.

[4]*Revue musicale*, December 1938, pp. 179–80.

[5]Vuillermoz et al., *Maurice Ravel par quelques-uns de ses familiers*, p. 60.

VOCALISE-ÉTUDE EN FORME DE HABANERA
(Vocalise-Etude in the Style of a Habanera; 1907)

This piece was commissioned by A. L. Hettich, a professor of voice at the Conservatoire, to introduce the students to contemporary vocal études. Many composers responded to Hettich's request, among them Gabriel Fauré, Arthur Honegger, Jacques Ibert, and Albert Roussel. Ravel's vocalization, which is underpinned by the habanera rhythm, gives the performer ample opportunity for display within a limited range of virtuosity. The composition later achieved considerable popularity in a violin transcription entitled *Pièce en forme de Habanera*, and thus for once the tables were turned on the master adapter of the art of others.

LES GRANDS VENTS VENUS D'OUTREMER (The Great Winds Coming from Beyond the Sea; poem by Henri de Régnier; 1907; dedicated to Jacques Durand; first performance: Hélène Luquiens and Ravel, June 8, 1907, Paris)

Ravel turned to the writings of Henri de Régnier (1864–1936) on three occasions. In addition to his setting of this symbolist poem, a quotation from the collection *La Cité des eaux* appears in the score of *Jeux d'eau*, and a phrase from the novel *Les Rencontres de Monsieur de Bréot* is found in the *Valses nobles et sentimentales*. "Les Grands Vents venus d'outremer" first appeared in a collection entitled *Tel qu'en songe* (1892). The pathos and violence of the poem are reasonably well matched by a turbulent, highly chromatic, and somewhat overcharged accompaniment, which is frequently quite independent of the vocal line. Ravel's setting is somewhat atypical, and the song occupies a relatively isolated position in the composer's catalogue.

SUR L'HERBE (On the Grass; poem by Paul Verlaine; 1907; first performance: Jane Bathori and Ravel, December 12, 1907, Paris)

In an unpublished letter to the critic Georges Jean-Aubry written on September 4, 1907, Ravel commented on *Sur l'herbe*: "In this piece, as in the *Histoires naturelles*, the impression must be given that one is almost not singing. A bit of preciosity is found there which is indicated moreover by the text and the music." The abbé's charming and incoherent comments, which include two allusions to music, are underscored by a graceful accompaniment, which evokes an eighteenth-century dance. The autograph of *Sur l'herbe* suggests that Ravel contemplated setting a series of poems from *Fêtes galantes*, but as it turned out the song proved to be his final adaptation of Verlaine's poetry.

CHANTS POPULAIRES (Folk Songs)
I. Chanson espagnole (Spanish song).
II. Chanson française (French song; gathered by Léon Branchet and Johannès Plantadis, this song was published in Paris by the Schola Cantorum in 1904).
III. Chanson italienne (Italian song).
IV. Chanson hébraïque (Hebraic song; gathered by Joel Engel in Vilna, Russia, in 1909).

In 1910, at the invitation of the Russian soprano Marie Olénine d'Alheim (1869–1970), Ravel participated in an international competition sponsored by the Maison du Lied in Moscow. The organization was founded with a threefold purpose in mind: first, to stimulate public interest in folk melodies; second, to increase the repertory of artistically harmonized folk melodies by inviting composers to enter biannual competitions; finally, to encourage young singers by giving them the opportunity to perform folk songs before the public in small recital halls. The competition entailed setting seven folk melodies (Spanish, Russian, Flemish, French, Scottish, Italian, and Hebraic). Ravel won first prize in four of the categories, and the other prizes were won by Alexander Olénine[1] (Russian song) and Alexandre Georges[2] (Flemish and Scottish songs).

Ravel's accompaniments are indicative of his broad empathies. The guitarlike accompaniment of the Spanish song effectively captures its bitter irony, while the French song is elegant and charming. The Italian song, dealing with the pangs of unrequited love, is the shortest and perhaps least successful of the group. The Hebraic song, a dialogue between father and son, is in Yiddish, Hebrew, and Aramaic; a dancelike section (the father's questions) alternates with recitative (the son's replies) in a simple, tasteful manner.

---

[1]Mme Olénine d'Alheim's brother, he was a student of Balakirev.

[2]A minor French composer of the day (1850–1938). Ravel's Flemish and Russian songs have not been recovered. His Scottish song was reconstructed by this writer on the basis of a sketch (Salabert, 1975). Based on a wistful love poem by Robert Burns ("The Banks o' Doon," 1791), it is an important addition to the collection.

TROIS POÈMES DE STÉPHANE MALLARMÉ (Three Poems by Stéphane Mallarmé)

I.   Soupir (Sigh); dedicated to Igor Stravinsky.
II. Placet futile (Futile Petition); dedicated to Florent Schmitt.
III. Surgi de la croupe et du bond (Rising from the Crupper and the Leap); dedicated to Erik Satie.
     (1913;[1] first performance: Jane Bathori, with a chamber ensemble[2] conducted by Désiré-Émile Inghelbrecht, January 14, 1914, Paris)

During the opening seasons of the Ballets Russes, in which *The Firebird*, *Petrushka*, and *Daphnis et Chloé* were presented, Ravel and Stravinsky occasionally attended rehearsals of each other's music. Their cordial relationship was to become even closer when they jointly accepted a commission from Serge Diaghilev to reorchestrate and adapt part of Mussorgsky's incomplete opera *Khovanshchina*. The composers worked on the assignment in Clarens, Switzerland, during March and April, 1913. In the course of their collaboration, Stravinsky showed his colleague the manuscript of his most recent ballet, *Le Sacre du printemps*. Ravel was extremely enthusiastic, and predicted in a letter to his friend Lucien Garban that the creation of *Le Sacre du printemps* would be an event as

important as the première of *Pelléas et Mélisande*. Another score that Ravel discovered at Clarens was Stravinsky's *Poèmes de la lyrique japonaise*, and he expressed considerable interest in the music, as well as its setting for solo voice accompanied by a chamber ensemble. Stravinsky explained that his instrumentation was derived from the score of *Pierrot lunaire*, which Schoenberg had recently shown him in Berlin. Though unacquainted with Schoenberg's work, Ravel was anxious to exploit its coloristic possibilities, and he soon completed "Soupir," the first of his Mallarmé poems. While Ravel was occupied with his settings of Mallarmé's poetry, Claude Debussy was composing his final homage to the poet, entitled *Trois Poèmes de Stéphane Mallarmé* (for voice and piano), and both collections were published by Durand about the same time. It was curious that both composers would independently set three poems by Mallarmé; when two of their three selections turned out to be identical, it was, as Debussy noted with dismay, a "phenomenon of autosuggestion worthy of communication to the Academy of Medicine." Ravel completed his songs before Debussy, and asked Dr. Edmond Bonniot, Mallarmé's son-in-law, for permission to utilize the poet's texts. The men were on friendly terms and the required authorization was granted immediately. A short time later, when Dr. Bonniot was approached by Jacques Durand with a similar request, he agreed to the publication of Debussy's "Éventail," but refused "Soupir" and "Placet futile," whose rights had just been granted to Ravel. Debussy's songs were published only after Ravel begged Dr. Bonniot to grant Durand the required authorization, a gesture typical of his probity and good will.

The poetry of Stéphane Mallarmé poses considerable intellectual challenge. Ravel once commented on the poet's "unbounded visions, yet precise in design, enclosed in a mystery of sombre abstractions—an art where all the elements are so intimately bound up together that one cannot analyze, but only sense its effect." On another occasion, he explained: "I wished to transpose Mallarmé's poetry, especially that preciosity so full of meaning and so characteristic of him. 'Surgi de la croupe et du bond' is the strangest, if not the most hermetic of his sonnets." In a letter to his colleague and biographer Roland-Manuel, written on October 7, 1913, Ravel discussed his setting of "Placet futile":

> . . . Just as your letter arrived I was finishing my 3 poems. Indeed, *Placet futile* was completed, but I retouched it. I fully realize the great audacity of having attempted to interpret this sonnet in music. It was necessary that the melodic contour, the modulations, and the rhythms be as precious, as properly contoured as the sentiment and the images of the text. Nevertheless, it was necessary to maintain the elegant deportment of the poem. Above all, it was necessary to maintain the profound and exquisite tenderness which suffuses all of this. Now that it's done, I'm a bit nervous about it.

Ravel's concern to maintain the "profound and exquisite tenderness" of the sonnet is of considerable interest, particularly in view of the fact that he was often maligned as a cerebral contriver of effects—as was Stéphane Mallarmé. The poet described "Soupir" as "an autumnal reverie," and on another occasion he observed that "Placet futile" was an evocation of a painting by Boucher or Watteau. "Surgi de la croupe et du bond," a difficult evocation of an empty vase, has been interpreted by a noted Mallarmé scholar as follows:

> The poet is alone and looking down at the empty vase as if he were a sylph painted on the ceiling. . . . No water is in the vase. It seems to be dying because of its emptiness. . . . The waiting of the vase for water is comparable to the waiting of the poet throughout the darkness of the night. A rose, placed in the opening of the vase, would have fulfilled the vase in its reason for being, as a poem or some act of creation would have justified the poet's vigil.[3]

Ravel's setting of the poem manages to match its verbal wizardry, primarily by exploiting a harmonic scheme that is not tonally oriented. The songs thus progress from traditional tonality ("Soupir") to a suggestion of atonality within a tonal framework ("Placet futile") to genuine atonality ("Surgi de la croupe et du bond"). Ravel never returned to the atonality of his concluding song, and it is a work of extraordinary interest. The Mallarmé poems occupy a rather isolated position in the composer's catalogue, and although relatively unknown, they constitute a superb achievement. As in the *Shéhérazade* cycle, the piano accompanist in the Mallarmé poems must attempt to capture the resplendent colors of the chamber ensemble.

---

[1]There are two complete autographs of the Mallarmé songs, one for voice and piano, the other for voice and instruments. The latter autograph (and the Durand edition) indicates the following: "Soupir," Clarens, April 2, 1913; "Placet futile," Paris, May, 1913; "Surgi de la croupe et du bond," St. Jean de Luz, August, 1913.

[2]The chamber ensemble consists of a piccolo, flute, clarinet, bass clarinet, string quartet, and piano.

[3]Wallace Fowlie, *Mallarmé* (Chicago: Univ. of Chicago Press, 1953), p. 51.

DEUX MÉLODIES HÉBRAÏQUES (Two Hebraic Songs)
I. Kaddisch (Kaddish).
II. L'Énigme éternelle (The Eternal Enigma; text and melody first published by the Society for Jewish Folk Music, Russia, 1911).
(1914;[1] dedicated to Madame Alvina-Alvi; first performance: Alvina-Alvi and Ravel, June 3, 1914, Paris)

The Hebraic melodies form an interesting contrast, with the rhapsodic cantorial melismas of the "Kaddisch" offset by the folklike simplicity of "L'Énigme éternelle." Although the latter text, in Yiddish, is of no particular import, the Aramaic text of the "Kaddisch" is one of the masterpieces of the Jewish liturgy. Abraham Idelsohn criticized Ravel's setting of "L'Énigme éternelle" as "ultramodern . . . without regard for its scale and the nature of the mode."[2] This observation was made in 1929, and today, of course, the accompaniment no longer appears "ultramodern." It should be pointed out that in all of his folk harmonizations, Ravel's sole concern was to write a tasteful accompaniment, and thus any restriction imposed upon his choice of harmony would have been totally unacceptable. The French texts of the Hebraic melodies were arranged by the composer, after he had been supplied with a literal translation. These songs form a natural pendant to the "Chanson hébraïque," and they marked Ravel's final adaptation of folk melodies.

---

[1]There is also Ravel's orchestral transcription (1919); first performance: Madeleine Grey, Rhené-Baton conducting the Pasdeloup Orchestra, April 17, 1920.

[2]Idelsohn, *Jewish Music in Its Historical Development* (New York: Henry Holt, 1929), p. 486. See also p. 490, example 5, for a "correct" harmonization of another version of the melody.

Suggestions for Further Reference

Bernac, Pierre. *The Interpretation of French Song*, 2nd ed. New York: W. W. Norton & Co., 1978.

Calvocoressi, M. D. *Musicians Gallery: Music and Ballet in Paris and London*. London: Faber & Faber, 1933.

Grubb, Thomas. *Singing in French*. New York: Schirmer Books, 1979.

Hopkins, G. W. "Maurice Ravel," in *The New Grove Twentieth-Century French Masters*. New York: W. W. Norton & Co., 1986, pp. 151–93.

Musical. "Ravel." Special issue, No. 4, June 1987.

Orenstein, Arbie. *A Ravel Reader*. New York: Columbia University Press, 1990.

Revue Musicale. "Maurice Ravel." Two special issues, April 1925 and December 1938.

Vuillermoz, Émile, et al. *Maurice Ravel par quelques-uns de ses familiers*. Paris: Éditions du Tambourinaire, 1939.

Ravel: *The Complete Songs* (with Orchestral, Chamber Ensemble or Piano Accompaniment). Gabriel Bacquier, baritone; Jessye Norman, soprano; and others. Dalton Baldwin, piano; Orchestre du Capitole de Toulouse; and Ensemble de Chambre de l'Orchestre de Paris. Conducted by Michel Plasson. 3 records: Angel DSCX-3965; 2 compact discs: Angel CDCB 47638.

Texts and Translations

SAINTE (Stéphane Mallarmé)

A la fenêtre recélant
Le santal vieux qui se dédore
De la viole étincelant
Jadis selon flûte ou mandore

Est la sainte pâle étalant
Le livre vieux qui se déplie
Du Magnificat ruisselant
Jadis selon vêpre ou complie

A ce vitrage d'ostensoir
Que frôle une harpe par l'Ange
Formée avec son vol du soir
Pour la délicate phalange

Du doigt que sans le vieux santal
Ni le vieux livre elle balance
Sur le plumage instrumental,
Musicienne du silence.

SAINT

At the window that harbors
The old flaking-gilt sandalwood
Of the viol that sparkled
In the past to flute or mandore

Is the pale female saint who displays
The old unfolding volume
Of the Magnificat that flowed
In the past for vespers or compline

At this monstrance-glass
Brushed by a harp that the Angel
Forms in his evening flight
For the delicate tip

Of the finger that, without the old sandalwood
Or the old book, she balances
On the instrumental plumage:
Musician of silence.

ÉPIGRAMMES DE CLÉMENT MAROT

D'Anne qui me jecta de la neige

Anne par jeu me jecta de la neige
Que je cuidoys froide certainement:
Mais c'estoit feu, l'expérience en ay-je
Car embrasé je fuz soubdainement
Puisque le feu loge secretement
Dedans la neige, où trouveray-je place
Pour n'ardre point? Anne, ta seule grâce
Estaindre peut le feu que je sens bien
Non point par eau, par neige, ne par glace,
Mais par sentir ung feu pareil au mien.

D'Anne jouant de l'espinette

Lorsque je voy en ordre la brunette
Jeune, en bon point, de la ligne des Dieux,
Et que sa voix, ses doits et l'espinette
Meinent ung bruyct doulx et melodieux,
J'ay du plaisir, et d'oreilles et d'yeulx

EPIGRAMS BY CLÉMENT MAROT

On Anne Throwing Snow at Me

Anne playfully threw snow at me
That I thought would surely be cold,
But it was fire—I felt it—
For I was suddenly set aflame.
Since fire lodges secretly
Within snow, where can I turn
To avoid burning? Anne, only your mercy
Can quench the fire I feel so keenly:
Not with water, with snow, nor with ice,
But by feeling a fire similar to mine.

On Anne Playing the Spinet

When I see the tidy dark-haired girl,
Young, plump, a descendant of the gods,
And when her voice, her fingers and the spinet
Produce a sweet and melodious sound,
I have more pleasure through my ears and eyes

Plus que les sainctz en leur gloire immortelle
Et autant qu'eulx je devien glorieux
Dès que je pense estre ung peu ayme d'elle.

Than the saints in their immortal glory,
And I become as glorious as they are
The moment I think myself a little beloved by her.

MANTEAU DE FLEURS (Paul Gravollet)

Toutes les fleurs de mon jardin sont roses,
Le rose sied à sa beauté.
Les primevères sont les premières écloses,
Puis viennent les tulipes et les jacinthes roses,
Les jolis œillets, les si belles roses,
Toute la variété des fleurs si roses
Du printemps et de l'été!
Le rose sied à sa beauté!
Toutes mes pivoines sont roses,
Roses aussi sont mes glaïeuls,
Roses mes géraniums; seuls,
Dans tout ce rose un peu troublant,
Les lys ont le droit d'être blancs.
Et quand elle passe au milieu des fleurs
Emperlées de rosée en pleurs,
Dans le parfum grisant des roses,
Et sous la caresse des choses
Toute grâce, amour, pureté!
Les fleurs lui font un manteau rose
Dont elle pare sa beauté.

MANTLE OF FLOWERS

All the flowers in my garden are pink;
Pink is becoming to her beauty.
The primroses are the first to bloom,
Then come the pink tulips and hyacinths,
The pretty carnations, the roses that are so beautiful,
The full variety of flowers so pink
Of spring and summer!
Pink is becoming to her beauty!
All my peonies are pink,
Pink too are my gladioli,
Pink my geraniums; alone
In all this somewhat disturbing pink,
The lilies have the right to be white.
And when she walks amid the flowers
That are pearled with weeping dew,
In the heady fragrance of the roses
And beneath the caress of nature,
The embodiment of grace, love, purity!
The flowers form a pink mantle for her
With which she adorns her beauty.

SHÉHÉRAZADE (Tristan Klingsor)

I. Asie

Asie, Asie, Asie.
Vieux pays merveilleux des contes de nourrice
Où dort la fantaisie comme une impératrice
En sa forêt tout emplie de mystère.
Asie,
Je voudrais m'en aller avec la goëlette
Qui se berce ce soir dans le port
Mystérieuse et solitaire
Et qui déploie enfin ses voiles violettes
Comme un immense oiseau de nuit dans le ciel d'or.
Je voudrais m'en aller vers des îles de fleurs
En écoutant chanter la mer perverse
Sur un vieux rythme ensorceleur.
Je voudrais voir Damas et les villes de Perse
Avec les minarets légers dans l'air.
Je voudrais voir de beaux turbans de soie
Sur des visages noirs aux dents claires;
Je voudrais voir des yeux sombres d'amour
Et des prunelles brillantes de joie
En des peaux jaunes comme des oranges;
Je voudrais voir des vêtements de velours
Et des habits à longues franges.
Je voudrais voir des calumets entre des bouches

SCHEHERAZADE

I. Asia

Asia, Asia, Asia.
Ancient wonderland of nursery tales,
Where imagination sleeps like an empress
In her forest all filled with mystery.
Asia,
I would like to depart on the schooner
That is rocking this evening in the harbor,
Mysterious and solitary,
And that finally unfurls its violet sails
Like a huge night bird in the golden sky.
I would like to depart for isles of flowers
While listening to the song of the perverse sea
With its ancient bewitching rhythm.
I would like to see Damascus and the cities of Persia
With their light minarets in the air.
I would like to see beautiful silk turbans
On black faces with gleaming teeth;
I would like to see eyes dark with love
And their pupils shining with joy
Set in skins yellow as oranges;
I would like to see velvet clothing
And garments with long fringes.
I would like to see calumets in mouths

Tout entourées de barbe blanche;
Je voudrais voir d'âpres marchands aux regards louches,
Et des cadis, et des vizirs
Qui du seul mouvement de leur doigt qui se penche
Accordent vie ou mort au gré de leur désir.
Je voudrais voir la Perse, et l'Inde, et puis la Chine,
Les mandarins ventrus sous les ombrelles,
Et les princesses aux mains fines,
Et les lettrés qui se querellent
Sur la poésie et sur la beauté;
Je voudrais m'attarder au palais enchanté
Et comme un voyageur étranger
Contempler à loisir des paysages peints
Sur des étoffes en des cadres de sapin
Avec un personnage au milieu d'un verger;
Je voudrais voir des assassins souriant
Du bourreau qui coupe un cou d'innocent
Avec son grand sabre courbé d'Orient.
Je voudrais voir des pauvres et des reines;
Je voudrais voir des roses et du sang;
Je voudrais voir mourir d'amour ou bien de haine.
Et puis m'en revenir plus tard
Narrer mon aventure aux curieux de rêves
En élevant comme Sindbad ma vieille tasse arabe
De temps en temps jusqu'à mes lèvres
Pour interrompre le conte avec art . . .

Completely encircled with white beards;
I would like to see ruthless merchants with shifty eyes,
And cadis and viziers
Who merely by moving their bent finger
Grant life or death according to their whim.
I would like to see Persia, and India, and then China.
The paunchy mandarins beneath parasols,
And the princesses with delicate hands,
And the scholars arguing
About poetry and beauty;
I would like to linger in an enchanted palace
And, like a foreign traveler,
Contemplate at leisure landscapes painted
On fabrics in pine frames
With a figure in the middle of an orchard;
I would like to see assassins smiling
As they watch the executioner cut through an innocent
    man's neck
With his big Oriental scimitar.
I would like to see paupers and queens;
I would like to see roses and blood;
I would like to see people dying of love or else of hatred.
And then return later on
To relate my adventure to connoisseurs of dreams,
Like Sinbad raising my old Arabic cup
To my lips from time to time
To interrupt my tale artfully . . .

II. La Flûte enchantée

L'ombre est douce et mon maître dort
Coiffé d'un bonnet conique de soie
Et son long nez jaune en sa barbe blanche.
Mais moi, je suis éveillée encor
Et j'écoute au dehors
Une chanson de flûte où s'épanche
Tour à tour la tristesse ou la joie.
Un air tour à tour langoureux ou frivole
Que mon amoureux chéri joue,
Et quand je m'approche de la croisée
Il me semble que chaque note s'envole
De la flûte vers ma joue
Comme un mystérieux baiser.

II. The Magic Flute

The shade is pleasant and my master is asleep,
Wearing a conical silken cap,
His long yellow nose buried in his white beard.
But I, I am still awake
And I listen
To a flute song outside expressing
Sadness and joy in turn.
A melody languid and frivolous in turn
Which my dearly beloved plays,
And when I approach the casement
I feel as if each note flies away
From the flute to my cheek
Like a mysterious kiss.

III. L'Indifférent

Tes yeux sont doux comme ceux d'une fille,
Jeune étranger,
Et la courbe fine
De ton beau visage de duvet ombragé
Est plus séduisante encor de ligne.
Ta lèvre chante sur le pas de ma porte
Une langue inconnue et charmante
Comme une musique fausse.
Entre!
Et que mon vin te réconforte . . .
Mais non, tu passes
Et de mon seuil je te vois t'éloigner
Me faisant un dernier geste avec grâce
Et la hanche légèrement ployée
Par ta démarche féminine et lasse . . .

III. The Unresponsive One

Your eyes are gentle like a girl's,
Young stranger,
And the delicate curve
Of your beautiful face shadowed with down
Has a line that is even more seductive.
Your lips sing on my doorstep
An unknown, charming language
Like music off-pitch.
Come in!
And let my wine refresh you . . .
But no, you walk by
And from my threshold I see you move away
Addressing a final graceful gesture to me,
Your hips slightly bent
By your feminine, languid gait . . .

CINQ MÉLODIES POPULAIRES GRECQUES
(translated from the Greek by Michel Dimitri Calvocoressi)

I. Chanson de la mariée

Réveille-toi, réveille-toi, perdrix mignonne, ouvre au matin tes ailes. Trois grains de beauté, mon cœur en est brûlé! Vois le ruban d'or que je t'apporte, pour le nouer autour de tes cheveux. Si tu veux, ma belle, viens nous marier! Dans nos deux familles, tous sont alliés!

II. Là-bas, vers l'église

Là-bas, vers l'église, vers l'église Ayio Sidéro, l'église, ô Vierge sainte, l'église Ayio Costanndino, se sont réunis, rassemblés en nombre infini, du monde, ô Vierge sainte, du monde tous les plus braves!

III. Quel Galant m'est comparable

Quel galant m'est comparable, d'entre ceux qu'on voit passer? Dis, dame Vassiliki? Vois, pendus à ma ceinture, pistolets et sabre aigu . . . Et c'est toi que j'aime!

IV. Chanson des cueilleuses de lentisques

O joie de mon âme, joie de mon cœur, trésor qui m'est si cher; joie de l'âme et du cœur, toi que j'aime ardemment, tu es plus beau qu'un ange. O lorsque tu parais, ange si doux devant nos yeux, comme un bel ange blond, sous le clair soleil, Hélas! tous nos pauvres cœurs soupirent!

V. Tout gai!

Tout gai! gai, Ha, tout gai! Belle jambe, tireli, qui danse; Belle jambe, la vaisselle danse, Tra la la la la . . .

FIVE GREEK FOLK SONGS

I. Bride's Song

Awake, awake, dainty partridge. Open your wings to the morning. Three beauty spots set my heart on fire! See the ribbon, the golden ribbon I bring you to tie around your hair. If you wish, lovely one, let us be married! In our two families everyone is related!

II. Yonder by the Church

Yonder by the church, by the church Ayio Sidero, the church—O Blessed Virgin—the church Ayio Constanndino, there are gathered, there are assembled in infinite numbers, the world's—O Blessed Virgin—all the world's best people!

III. What Gallant Can Be Compared with Me

What gallant can be compared with me of all those one sees passing by? Tell me, lady Vassiliki? See the pistol and sharp sword attached to my belt . . . And it's you that I love!

IV. Song of the Girls Collecting Mastic

O joy of my soul, joy of my heart, treasure so dear to me; joy of my soul and heart, whom I love ardently, you are handsomer than an angel. Oh, when you appear, angel so sweet, before our eyes, like a handsome blond angel, in the bright sunshine, alas! all our poor hearts sigh.

V. Be Gay!

Be gay! gay, ha, be gay! Beautiful legs, tra la, dancing, beautiful legs, the dishes are dancing too, tra la la la la . . .

NOËL DES JOUETS (Maurice Ravel)

Le troupeau verni des moutons
Roule en tumulte vers la crèche
Les lapins tambours, brefs et rêches,
Couvrent leurs aigres mirlitons.
Vierge Marie, en crinoline.
Ses yeux d'émail sans cesse ouverts,
En attendant Bonhomme hiver
Veille Jésus qui se dodine.
Car, près de là, sous un sapin,
Furtif, emmitouflé dans l'ombre
Du bois, Belzébuth, le chien sombre,
Guette l'Enfant de sucre peint.
Mais les beaux anges incassables
Suspendus par des fils d'archal
Du haut de l'arbuste hiémal
Assurent la paix des étables.
Et leur vol de clinquant vermeil
Qui cliquette en bruits symétriques
S'accorde au bétail mécanique
Dont la voix grêle bêle:
"Noël! Noël! Noël!"

THE TOYS' CHRISTMAS

The varnished flock of sheep
Rolls tumultuously toward the manger.
The drumming rabbits, curt and harsh,
Cover their shrill mirlitons.
The Virgin Mary, in crinoline,
Her enamel eyes unceasingly open,
Waiting for Father Christmas,
Watches over Jesus as she rocks him.
For nearby, under a fir tree,
Stealthy, wrapped in the shadow
Of the woods, Beelzebub, the sinister dog,
Lies in wait for the Child of tinted sugar.
But the beautiful, unbreakable angels,
Hanging by brass wires
From the top of the Christmas tree,
Guarantee the peace of the stables.
And their wings of vermilion tinsel,
Clicking in symmetrical sounds,
Harmonize with the mechanical livestock
Whose thin voices bleat:
"Noel! Noel! Noel!"

HISTOIRES NATURELLES (Jules Renard)

I. Le Paon

Il va sûrement se marier aujourd'hui. Ce devait être pour hier. En habit de gala, il était prêt. Il n'attendait que sa fiancée. Elle n'est pas venue. Elle ne peut tarder. Glorieux, il se promène avec une allure de prince indien et porte sur lui les riches présents d'usage. L'amour avive l'éclat de ses couleurs et son aigrette tremble comme une lyre. La fiancée n'arrive pas. Il monte au haut du toit et regarde du côté du soleil. Il jette son cri diabolique: Léon! Léon! C'est ainsi qu'il appelle sa fiancée. Il ne voit rien venir et personne ne répond. Les volailles habituées ne lèvent même point la tête. Elles sont lasses de l'admirer. Il redescend dans la cour, si sûr d'être beau qu'il est incapable de rancune. Son mariage sera pour demain. Et, ne sachant que faire du reste de la journée, il se dirige vers le perron. Il gravit les marches, comme des marches de temple, d'un pas officiel. Il relève sa robe à queue toute lourde des yeux qui n'ont pu se détacher d'elle. Il répète encore une fois la cérémonie.

II. Le Grillon

C'est l'heure où, las d'errer, l'insecte nègre revient de promenade et répare avec soin le désordre de son domaine. D'abord il ratisse ses étroites allées de sable. Il fait du bran de scie qu'il écarte au seuil de sa retraite. Il lime la racine de cette grande herbe propre à le harceler. Il se repose. Puis il remonte sa minuscule montre. A-t-il fini? est-elle cassée? Il se repose encore un peu. Il rentre chez lui et ferme sa porte. Longtemps il tourne sa clef dans la serrure délicate. Et il écoute: Point d'alarme dehors. Mais il ne se trouve pas en sûreté. Et comme par une chaînette dont la poulie grince, il descend jusqu'au fond de la terre. On n'entend plus rien. Dans la campagne muette, les peupliers se dressent comme des doigts en l'air et désignent la lune.

III. Le Cygne

Il glisse sur le bassin, comme un traîneau blanc, de nuage en nuage. Car il n'a faim que des nuages floconneux qu'il voit naître, bouger, et se perdre dans l'eau. C'est l'un d'eux qu'il désire. Il le vise du bec, et il plonge tout à coup son col vêtu de neige. Puis, tel un bras de femme sort d'une manche, il le retire. Il n'a rien. Il regarde: les nuages effarouchés ont disparu. Il ne reste qu'un instant désabusé, car les nuages tardent peu à revenir, et, là-bas, où meurent les ondulations de l'eau, en voici un qui se reforme. Doucement, sur son léger coussin de plumes, le cygne rame et s'approche . . . Il s'épuise à pêcher de vains reflets, et peut-être qu'il mourra, victime de cette illusion, avant d'attraper un seul morceau de nuage. Mais qu'est-ce que je dis? Chaque fois qu'il plonge, il fouille du bec la vase nourrissante et ramène un ver. Il engraisse comme une oie.

NATURAL HISTORIES

I. The Peacock

He will surely get married today. It was to have been yesterday. He was in full dress and ready. He was only waiting for his bride. She didn't come. She won't be long now. In his conceit, he struts about with the air of an Indian prince and wears the customary rich presents. Love heightens the brightness of his colors and his aigrette trembles like a lyre. His bride doesn't show up. He ascends to the roof and looks toward the sun. He utters his diabolical cry: "Léon! Léon!" That's what he calls his bride. He sees nothing coming and no one answers. The chickens, who are used to it, don't even raise their heads. They are tired of admiring him. He comes down to the yard again, so sure of being handsome that he is incapable of bearing a grudge. His wedding will take place tomorrow. And, not knowing what to do with the rest of the day, he heads for the stairway to the house. He climbs the steps, as if they were temple steps, with an official gait. He lifts his robe, with its train that is so weighed down with eyes that were unable to tear themselves away from it. He repeats the ceremony once again.

II. The Cricket

It is the hour when, tired of straying, the black insect returns from his outing and carefully puts his property back in shape. First he rakes his narrow lanes of sand. He makes sawdust, which he scatters onto the threshold of his shelter. He files down the root of that tall blade of grass that might annoy him. He rests. Then he winds up his tiny watch. Has he finished? Is it broken? He rests once again. He goes back into his house and closes the door. For a long while he turns the key in the delicate lock. And he listens: No noise outside. But he is still not safe. And, as if on a tiny chain with a squeaking pulley, he lowers himself to the heart of the earth. Nothing more is heard. In the silent countryside, the poplars rise straight up in the air like fingers and point to the moon.

III. The Swan

He glides on the pond, like a white sleigh, from cloud to cloud. For his hunger is only for the fleecy clouds that he sees forming, moving and being lost in the water. It is one of them that he desires. He aims at it with his beak, and suddenly immerses his snow-clad neck. Then, just as a woman's arm emerges from a sleeve, he pulls it back. He has caught nothing. He looks: The startled clouds have disappeared. He remains disillusioned for only a moment, for the clouds return before very long, and, over there, where the ripples on the water are dying away, one cloud is already forming. Softly, on his light feather cushion, the swan paddles and approaches . . . He exhausts himself fishing for empty reflections, and perhaps he will die, a victim to that illusion, before catching a single piece of cloud. But what am I talking about? Every time he dives, he burrows in the nourishing mud with his beak and comes back with a worm. He's fattening up like a goose.

IV. Le Martin-Pêcheur

Ça n'a pas mordu, ce soir, mais je rapporte une rare émotion. Comme je tenais ma perche de ligne tendue, un martin-pêcheur est venu s'y poser. Nous n'avons pas d'oiseau plus éclatant. Il semblait une grosse fleur bleue au bout d'une longue tige. La perche pliait sous le poids. Je ne respirais plus, tout fier d'être pris pour un arbre par un martin-pêcheur. Et je suis sûr qu'il ne s'est pas envolé de peur, mais qu'il a cru qu'il ne faisait que passer d'une branche à une autre.

V. La Pintade

C'est la bossue de ma cour. Elle ne rêve que plaies à cause de sa bosse. Les poules ne lui disent rien: Brusquement, elle se précipite et les harcèle. Puis elle baisse sa tête, penche le corps, et, de toute la vitesse de ses pattes maigres, elle court frapper, de son bec dur, juste au centre de la roue d'une dinde. Cette poseuse l'agaçait. Ainsi, la tête bleue, ses barbillons à vif, cocardière, elle rage du matin au soir. Elle se bat sans motif, peut-être parce qu'elle s'imagine toujours qu'on se moque de sa taille, de son crâne chauve et de sa queue basse. Et elle ne cesse de jeter un cri discordant qui perce l'air comme une pointe. Parfois elle quitte la cour et disparaît. Elle laisse aux volailles pacifiques un moment de répit. Mais elle revient plus turbulente et plus criarde. Et, frénétique, elle se vautre par terre. Qu'a-t-elle donc? La sournoise fait une farce. Elle est allée pondre son œuf à la campagne. Je peux le chercher si ça m'amuse. Et elle se roule dans la poussière comme une bossue.

IV. The Kingfisher

Not a bite this evening, but I had a rare emotional experience. As I was holding my fishing rod out, a kingfisher came and perched on it. We have no other bird so striking. It resembled a big blue flower at the tip of a long stem. The rod bent beneath its weight. I held my breath, very proud of being taken for a tree by a kingfisher. And I'm sure that it didn't fly away out of fear, but in the belief that it was merely passing from one branch to another.

V. The Guinea Fowl

She is the hunchback of my barnyard. She is always ready for a fight because of her hump. She doesn't care for the hens: She suddenly leaps forward and harries them. Then she lowers her head, bends her body, and, with all the speed her skinny legs can muster, dashes over to bite with her hard beak right at the center of a turkey hen's out-spread tail. That affected creature got her goat. Thus, her head blued, her wattles raw, blustery, she rages from morning to evening. She fights without a reason, perhaps because she always imagines that someone is making fun of her shape, her bald crown and her low tail. And she incessantly utters a discordant cry that pierces the air like a knife point. Sometimes she leaves the yard and vanishes. She grants the peace-loving fowl a moment of respite. But she returns more unruly and noisy. And, in a frenzy, she wallows on the ground. What's wrong with her? The sneak is playing a trick. She went out into the countryside to lay an egg. I can go look for it if I feel so inclined. And she rolls in the dust like a hunchback.

LES GRANDS VENTS VENUS D'OUTREMER
(Henri de Régnier)

Les grands vents venus d'outremer
Passent par la ville, l'hiver,
Comme des étrangers amers.

Ils se concertent, graves et pâles,
Sur les places, et leurs sandales
Ensablent le marbre des dalles.

Comme de crosses à leurs mains fortes,
Ils heurtent l'auvent et la porte
Derrière qui l'horloge est morte.

Et les adolescents amers
S'en vont avec eux vers la mer.

THE GREAT WINDS COMING FROM BEYOND THE SEA

The great winds coming from beyond the sea
Pass through the city in wintertime
Like bitter strangers.

Solemn and pale, they scheme together
In the squares, and their sandals
Spread sand over the marble of the flagstones.

As if with rifle butts in their strong hands,
They batter the porch roof and the door
Behind which the clock has died.

And the bitter adolescents
Go off with them toward the sea.

SUR L'HERBE (Paul Verlaine)

L'abbé divague. —Et toi, marquis,
Tu mets de travers ta perruque.
—Ce vieux vin de Chypre est exquis;
Moins, Camargo, que votre nuque.

ON THE GRASS

The abbé rambles on: "And you, Marquis,
You're putting your wig on crooked."
"This old Cyprus wine is exquisite;
But less so than your nape, Camargo."[1]

—Ma flamme . . . Do, mi, sol, la, si.
—L'abbé, ta noirceur se dévoile.
—Que je meure, mesdames, si
Je ne vous décroche une étoile.

—Je voudrais être petit chien!
Embrassons nos bergères, l'une
Après l'autre, Messieurs, eh bien?
Do, mi, sol, Hé! bonsoir la Lune!

"My love . . . do, mi, sol, la, ti."
"Abbé, you are revealing your baseness."
"May I die, ladies, if
I don't bring down a star for you."

"I'd like to be a lapdog!
Let's kiss our shepherdesses, one
After the other, gentlemen, well?
Do, mi, sol. Hey! Good evening, Moon!"

----

[1]Marie Camargo, an eighteenth-century ballerina.

CHANTS POPULAIRES

Chanson espagnole

FRENCH:
Adieu, va, mon homme, adieu,
Puisqu'ils t'ont pris pour la guerre
Il n'est desormais sur terre,
Las! pour moi ni ris, ni jeu!
La, la, la, . . .

Castille prend nos garçons
Pour fair(e) triompher sa cause,
S'en vont aussi doux que roses,
Reviennent durs com(me) chardons.
La, la, la, . . .

GALICIAN:
Adios meu homiño, adios,
Ja qui te marchas pr'a guerra
Non t'olvides d'aprendina
Quiche qued' a can'a terra.
La, la, la, . . .

Castellanos de Castilla
Tratade ben os gallegos:
Cando van, van como rosas,
Cando ven, ven como negros.
La, la, la, . . .

Chanson française

FRENCH:
Jeanneton où irons-nous garder,
Qu'ayons bon [temps] une heure? Lan la!
Là-bas, là-bas, au pré barré,
Y'a de tant belles ombres Lan la!

Le pastour quitte son manteau,
Et fait seoir Jeannette Lan la!
Jeannette a tellement joué,
Que s'y est oubliée, Lan la!

LIMOUSIN:
Janeta ount anirem gardar,
Qu'ajam boun tems un' oura? Lan la!
Aval, aval, al prat barrat;
Ia de tan belas oumbras! Lan la!

Lou pastour quita soun mantel,
Per far sieire Janeta Lan la!
Janeta a talamen jougat,
Que se ies oublidada, Lan la!

FOLK SONGS

Spanish Song

TRANSLATION OF FRENCH:
Farewell, my husband, farewell;
Since they have taken you for the war
There is no longer on earth,
Alas! laughter or gaiety for me!
La, la, la . . .

Castille takes our young men
To aid in the triumph of its cause;
They leave as gentle as roses
And return as tough as thistles.
La, la, la . . .

TRANSLATION OF GALICIAN:
Farewell, my husband, farewell.
Now that you are leaving for the war,
Don't forget to be in touch with those
Who are staying behind in this country.
La, la, la . . .

Castilians of Castille,
Treat the Galicians well:
When they leave, they leave like roses;
When they return, they return like blacks.
La, la, la . . .

French Song

(THE FRENCH AND LIMOUSIN TEXTS ARE IDENTICAL IN MEANING)
"Jeannette, where shall we tend our sheep,
To have an hour's good time? Hey ho!"
"Down there in the gated meadow
There is plenty of lovely shade. Hey ho!"

The shepherd takes off his cloak
And sits Jeannette down. Hey ho!
Jeannette played so much
That she forgot herself! Hey ho!

Chanson italienne

FRENCH:

Penchée à ma fenêtre, j'écoute l'onde,
J'écoute ma misère si profonde!
Je clame mon amour, nul qui réponde!

ROMAN:

M'affaccio la finestra e vedo l'onde,
Vedo le mi[e] miserie che sò granne.
Chiamo l'amore mio, nun m'arrisponde.

Italian Song

TRANSLATION OF FRENCH:

Leaning on my windowsill, I listen to the waves,
I listen to my sorrow, which is so deep!
I pour out my love; there is no one to answer.

TRANSLATION OF ITALIAN (ROMAN):

I look out the window and see the waves,
I see my sorrows, which are great.
I call my sweetheart, but no one answers.

Chanson hébraïque

FRENCH:

Mayerke, mon fils, ô Mayerke, mon fils,
Devant qui te trouves-tu là?
Devant lui, Roi des Rois, et seul Roi, père mien,
Mayerke, mon fils, ô Mayerke, mon fils,
Et que lui demandes-tu là?
Des enfants, longue vie et mon pain, père mien.
Mayerke, mon fils, ô Mayerke, mon fils,
Mais me dis, pourquoi des enfants?
Aux enfants on apprend la Thora, père mien.
Mayerke, mon fils, ô Mayerke, mon fils,
Mais me dis, pourquoi longue vie?
Ce qui vit chante gloire au Seigneur, père mien.
Mayerke, mon fils, ô Mayerke, mon fils,
Mais tu veux encore du pain?
Prends ce pain, nourris-toi, bénis-le, père mien.

Hebraic Song

TRANSLATION OF FRENCH:

"Mayerke, my son, O Mayerke, my son,
In whose presence are you there?"
"In the presence of Him, King of Kings, and sole King, my
    father."
"Mayerke, my son, O Mayerke, my son,
And what are you asking him for?"
"For children, long life and my bread, my father."
"Mayerke, my son, O Mayerke, my son,
Tell me, why for children?"
"One teaches children Torah, my father."
"Mayerke, my son, O Mayerke, my son,
Tell me, why for long life?"
"That which lives sings the Lord's glory, my father."
"Mayerke, my son, O Mayerke, my son,
You want bread as well?"
"Take this bread, eat it, bless it, my father."

YIDDISH/ARAMAIC/HEBREW:

Mejerke, main Suhn, oi Mejerke, main Suhn,
Zi weiss tu, var wemen du steihst?
"Lifnei Melech Malchei hamlochim," Tatunju.
Mejerke, main Suhn, oi Mejerke, main Suhn,
Wos ze westu bai Ihm bet'n?
"Bonej, chajei, M'sunei," Tatunju.
Mejerke, main Suhn, oi Mejerke, main Suhn,
Oif wos darfs tu Bonei?
"Bonim eiskim batoiroh," Tatunju.
Mejerke, main Suhn, oi Mejerke, main Suhn,
Oif wos darfs tu chajei?
"Kol chai joiducho," Tatunju.
Mejerke, main Suhn, oi Mejerke, main Suhn,
Oif wo darfs tu M'sunei?
"W'ochalto w'sowoto uweirachto," Tatunju.

TRANSLATION OF HEBRAIC TEXT:

"Mayerke, my son, O Mayerke, my son,
Do you know before Whom you stand?"
" 'Before the King of the King of Kings,' dear father."
"Mayerke, my son, O Mayerke, my son,
What will you ask of Him?"
" 'Children, life, and sustenance,' dear father."
"Mayerke, my son, O Mayerke, my son,
For what do you need children?"
" 'Children to study the Torah,' dear father."
"Mayerke, my son, O Mayerke, my son,
For what do you need life?"
" 'All life shall praise Him,' dear father."
"Mayerke, my son, O Mayerke, my son,
For what do you need sustenance?"
" 'You shall eat, and be satisfied and bless [the Lord your
    God],'[1] dear father."

---

[1] Deuteronomy 8:10.

TROIS POÈMES DE STÉPHANE MALLARMÉ

I. Soupir

Mon âme vers ton front où rêve, ô calme sœur,
Un automne jonché de taches de rousseur
Et vers le ciel errant de ton œil angélique
Monte, comme dans un jardin mélancolique,
Fidèle, un blanc jet d'eau soupire vers l'Azur!
Vers l'Azur attendri d'Octobre pâle et pur
Qui mire aux grands bassins sa langueur infinie
Et laisse, sur l'eau morte où la fauve agonie
Des feuilles erre au vent et creuse un froid sillon,
Se traîner le soleil jaune d'un long rayon.

II. Placet futile

Princesse! à jalouser le destin d'une Hébé
Qui poind sur cette tasse au baiser de vos lèvres
J'use mes feux mais n'ai rang discret qui d'abbé
Et ne figurerai même nu sur le Sèvres.

Comme je ne suis pas ton bichon embarbé,
Ni la pastille, ni du rouge, ni jeux mièvres,
Et que sur moi je sais ton regard clos tombé,
Blonde dont les coiffeurs divins sont des orfèvres!

Nommez-nous . . . toi de qui tant de ris framboisés
Se joignent en troupeaux d'agneaux apprivoisés
Chez tous broutant les vœux et bêlant aux délires,

Nommez-nous . . . pour qu'Amour ailé d'un éventail
M'y peigne flûte aux doigts endormant ce bercail,
Princesse, nommez-nous berger de vos sourires.

III. Surgi de la croupe et du bond

Surgi de la croupe et du bond
D'une verrerie éphémère
Sans fleurir la veillée amère
Le col ignoré s'interrompt.

Je crois bien que deux bouches n'ont
Bu, ni son amant ni ma mère
Jamais à la même chimère
Moi, sylphe de ce froid plafond!

Le pur vase d'aucun breuvage
Que l'inexhaustible veuvage
Agonise mais ne consent,
Naïf baiser des plus funèbres!

A rien expirer annonçant
Une rose dans les ténèbres.

THREE POEMS BY STÉPHANE MALLARMÉ

I. Sigh

My soul rises toward your brow, O calm sister, where there
    lies dreaming
An autumn strewn with russet freckles,
And toward the restless sky of your angelic eye,
As in a melancholy garden,
A white fountain faithfully sighs toward the Azure!
Toward the compassionate Azure of pale and pure
    October,
Which mirrors its infinite languor in the great pools
And, on the stagnant water where the tawny agony
Of the leaves stirs in the wind and digs a cold furrow,
Lets the yellow sun drag itself out in a long ray.

II. Futile Petition

Princess! in envying the fate of a Hebe,[1]
Who appears on this cup at the kiss of your lips,
I use up my ardor, but my modest station is only that of
    abbé
And I won't even appear nude on the Sèvres porcelain.

Since I am not your bewhiskered lapdog,
Nor lozenge, nor rouge, nor affected games,
And since I know that you look on me with indifferent
    eyes,
Blonde whose divine hairdressers are goldsmiths!—

Appoint me . . . you whose many raspberried laughs
Are gathered into flocks of docile lambs,
Nibbling at all vows and bleating deliriously,

Appoint me . . . in order that Love, with a fan as his
    wings,
May paint me fingering a flute and lulling this sheepfold,
Princess, appoint me shepherd of your smiles.

---

[1] The gods' cupbearer.

III. Rising from the Crupper and the Leap

Rising from the crupper and the leap
Of an ephemeral piece of glassware,
Without adorning the bitter vigil with flowers,
The neglected neck stops short.

I do believe that two mouths have not
Drunk, neither her lover nor my mother,
Ever from the same chimera,
I, sylph of this cold ceiling!

The vase pure of any liquid
Except inexhaustible widowhood
Is on the verge of death but does not consent—
Naive, most funereal kiss—

To exhale any annunciation of
A rose in the darkness.

DEUX MÉLODIES HÉBRAÏQUES

I. Kaddisch

FRENCH:

Que ta gloire, ô Roi des rois, soit exaltée, ô toi qui dois renouveler le Monde et ressuciter les trépassés Ton règne, Adonaï, soit proclamé par nous, fils d'Israël, aujourd'hui, demain, à jamais. Disons tous: Amen. Qu'il soit aimé, qu'il soit chéri, qu'il soit loué, glorifié ton nom radieux. Qu'il soit béni, sanctifié; qu'il soit adoré, ton nom qui plane sur les cieux, sur nos louanges, sur nos hymnes, sur toutes nos bénédictions. Que le ciel clément nous accorde la vie calme, la paix, le bonheur. Ah! ah! ah! ah! ah! Disons tous: Amen.

ARAMAIC:

Yithgaddal weyithkaddash scheméh rabba be'olmâ diverâ 'khire'outhé veyamli'kh mal'khouté behayyé'khôn, ouveyome'khôn ouve'hayyé de'khol beth yisraël ba'agalâ ouvizman qariw weimrou. Amen. Yithbara'kh, we-yischtaba'h weyithpaêr weyithromam weyithnassé weyithhaddar weyith'allé weyithhallal scheméh de-qoudschâ beri'kh hou. Le'êlà min kol bir'khatha weschiratha touschbehatha wene'hamathâ daamirân ah! be'olma ah! ah! ah! ah! ah! Weïmrou Amen.

II. L'Énigme éternelle

FRENCH:

Monde tu nous interroges:
Tra la tra la la la la
L'on répond:
Tra la la . . .
Si l'on ne peut te répondre:
Tra la la . . .
Monde tu nous interroges:
Tra la la . . .

YIDDISH:

Frägt die Velt die alte Casche
Tra la tra la la la la
Entfernt men
Tra la la . . .
Un as men will kennen sagen
Tra la la . . .
Frägt die Velt die alte Casche
Tra la la . . .

TWO HEBRAIC SONGS

I. Kaddish (doxology)

TRANSLATION OF FRENCH:

May Your glory be exalted, O King of kings, O You who renew the world and resurrect the dead.

May Your reign, Lord, be proclaimed by us, the children of Israel, today, tomorrow, forever.

Let us all say: Amen.

May Your radiant name be adored, cherished, praised, and glorified.

May Your name be blessed, sanctified, exalted, Your name which is above the heavens, above our praises, above our hymns, above all our benedictions.

May merciful heaven grant us tranquility, peace, happiness.

Ah! Let us all say: Amen.

TRANSLATION OF ARAMAIC:

May His great name be magnified and hallowed in the world that He created according to His will.

And may He reign over His kingdom in your lifetime and in your days and in the lifetime of the entire house of Israel, speedily in our day.

And let us say Amen.

May the holy name be blessed and lauded, glorified and uplifted, extolled, honored, magnified, and praised.

Blessed is He, higher than all blessing and hymn, praise and consolation that are spoken in this world.

Ah![1] And let us say Amen.

---

[1] Does not appear in the original text of the Kaddish.

II. The Eternal Enigma

TRANSLATION OF FRENCH:

World, you ask us:
Tra la . . .
People reply:
Tra la . . .
If people cannot reply to you:
Tra la . . .
World, you ask us:
Tra la . . .

TRANSLATION OF YIDDISH:

The world asks the old question:
Tra la . . .
People reply:
Tra la . . .
And when people say:
Tra la . . .
The world asks the old question:
Tra la . . .

Glossary of French Terms

à, to, *à volonté*, freely, ad libitum
(en) accélérant, becoming faster
acc^t de piano, piano accompaniment
afféterie, affectation
agité, agitated
animé, animatedly, *animez*, becoming faster
Août, August
après, after
assez, rather
au, at the
aucune, any
avec, with
Avril, April
beaucoup, very, very much
bien, quite
calme, serenely
cédez, slower
chant, voice
clavecin, harpsichord
concours, competition
Corde, string, *1 Corde*, soft pedal, *3 Cordes*, soft pedal off
court, short
de, by, of
début, beginning
(en) dehors, prominently
doux, tenderly, sweetly
d'un, with a
en, in, *en dehors*, prominently
encore, still, again
enveloppé, enveloped, *enveloppé de pédales*, making full use of both pedals
et, and
expressif, expressively
fausset, falsetto
fin, end
fort, energetically
grave, solemn
harmonisation, harmonization
hâte, haste
imperceptiblement, imperceptibly
indolence, indolence
innocemment, innocently
jusqu'à, until, *jusqu'au*, until the
la, le, the
léger, light, *légèrement, leg^t*, lightly, slightly

lent, slow
liturgiquement, liturgically
lointain, distant
Mai, May
majesté, majesty
marqué, marcato
même, same
modéré, modérément, moderato, moderately
moins, less
Moscou, Moscow
mouvement, tempo, *1er mouvement, au Mouv^t*, tempo primo
musique, music
noblement, nobly
nuance, nuance, variation
on, one, *on ne peut plus lent*, as slow as possible
ou, or
par, by
pas, not
pédales, pedals
(en se) perdant, dying away
peu, little, *peu à peu*, gradually, *un peu*, a little
placide, placid
plus, more, *de plus en plus*, more and more
poésie, poetry
portez, portamento
précis, precise
presque, almost, *presqu'au mouv^t*, almost tempo primo
pressez, accelerando
primée, awarded the prize
progressivement, steadily
qu'au, than at the
rageusement, furiously
ralenti, ralentir, (en) ralentissant, ralentissez, rallentando, slowing
rapide, quickly
reprenez, resuming
respirer, taking a breath
retenez, slowing
retenu, held back
Romaine, Roman (dialect)
rythme, rhythm
sans, without
sec, dry
simplement, simply
solennel, solemnly

(en) sourdine, soft pedal, muted
subitement, suddenly
suivez, follow (the voice), colla voce
tendre, tenderly
toujours, always
tous le temps, continuously
traduction française, French translation

traînez, portamento, slurred
très, very
vite, fast
voix, voice
(à) volonté, freely, ad libitum
5e, fifth

SAINTE

Poésie de
STÉPHANE MALLARMÉ

Musique de
MAURICE RAVEL
(1896)

A la fe_nê_tre re_cé_lant Le san_tal vieux qui se dé_do_re De la vi_ole é_tin_ce_lant Ja_dis se_lon flûte ou man_dore

Original key in manuscript: F minor (see frontispiece); key of song as originally published: G minor.

Est la sain-te pâle é-ta-lant Le li-vre vieux qui se dé-pli-e Du Ma-gni-fi-cat ruis-se-lant Ja-dis se-lon vêpre ou com-plie A ce vi-tra-ge d'os-ten-soir Que frôle u-ne har-pe par l'An-ge For-mée a-vec son vol du

soir _____ Pour la dé _ li _ ca _ té pha _ lan _ _ _

_ge Du doigt que sans le vieux san _ tal Ni le vieux livre _____

_ el _ le ba _ lan _ ce Sur le plu _ mage ins _ tru _ men _ tal _____

Mu _ si _ ci _ en _ ne ___ du si _ lence. _____

Épigrammes de Clément Marot

à M. Hardy Thé.

D'ANNE QUI ME JECTA DE LA NEIGE.

MUSIQUE DE MAURICE RAVEL.

An - ne par jeu me jec-ta de la nei - - ge Que je

cui-doys froi-de cer-tai-nement:

Mais c'estoit

4

feu, l'ex - pé - rien - ce en ay _ je Car

em - bra - sé je fuz soub - dai - ne - ment

Puis - que le feu lo - ge se - cre - te -

ment De - dans la nei - ge, où trou - ve - ray - je pla - ce

Pour n'ardre point? An — ne, ta seu-le grâ-ce Es - tain-

dre peut le feu que je sens bien Non point par eau, par nei-ge,— ne par

gla — ce Mais par sen — tir ung-feu pa-reil au -

mien.

1ᵉʳ Mouvement.

à M. Hardy-Thé.

D'ANNE JOUANT DE L'ESPINETTE.

MUSIQUE DE MAURICE RAVEL.

7

voy en ordre la brunet-te Jeu-ne en bon point, de la li-gne des Dieux,

Et que sa voix, ses doits et l'es-pi-net-te

Meinent ung brüyct doulx et me-lo-di-eux

J'ay du plai-sir, et d'o-reil-les et d'y-eulx

8

Plus que les sainctz en leur gloire im - mor - tel - - le

Et autant qu'eulx je de - vien glo - ri - eux Dès que je

pen - - see streu ng peu ayme de'l - le.

Lent. 1er Mouvement.

19.
Manteau de Fleurs.

Poésie de Paul Gravollet.

Musique de Maurice Ravel.
(1903)

Tou-tes les fleurs de mon jar-din sont ro - - ses, Le ro-se sied à sa beau-té. Les pri-me-vè-res sont les pre-miè-res é-clo-ses, Puis vien-nent les tu - li-pes et les ja-cin-thes ro - - ses,

-si sont mes gla-ïeuls, Ro - ses mes gé-ra - niums; seuls,

Dans tout ce ro-se un peu trou-blant, Les lys ont le droit d'ê-tre blancs.

Et quand el-le pas-se au mi-lieu des fleurs Em-per - lées de ro-sée en pleurs, Dans le par -

-fum gri-sant des ro-ses, Et sous la ca-res-se des cho-ses

Tou-te grâce, a-mour, pu-re-té! _____ Les

fleurs lui font un man-teau ro-se Dont el-le pa-re sa beau-

Encore plus lent.

-té.

SHÉHÉRAZADE

Trois Poèmes de TRISTAN KLINGSOR

I
Asie

à Mademoiselle JEANE HATTO

MAURICE RAVEL

_rice Où dort la fantaisie comme une impé_ra _ trice En sa fo_ rêt tout emplie de mys_

_tè _ re.

Plus lent (♪=96)

Asie,

Je voudrais m'en al_ler a_vec la go_ë_let_te Qui se

ber_ce ce soir dans le port Mys_té_ri_euse et so_li_

_tai_re Et qui dé_

_ploie en_fin ses voi_les vi_o_let_tes Comme un im_

mense oi seau de nuit, dans le ciel d'or.

Un peu plus vite (♩.=50)

Je voudrais m'en al _ ler vers des î _ les de

fleurs _____ En é _ cou_

_tant chan _ _ter _____ la mer per _ ver _ se Sur un vieux

rythme en_sor_ce_leur.

Allegro (♪.=76)

Je vou'drais voir Da _

_mas et les vil_les de Perse a_vec les mi_na_rets lé _ gers dans

l'air.

Je vou_drais

en dehors

voir   de beaux turbans de   soie   Sur des vi_sa_ges   noirs   aux   dents

clai _ _ res;

dim. _ _ _ e

rall. _ _ _ _ _ (♩=60)
Lent

Je vou_drais   voir   des yeux sombres d'a_

_mour Et des prunel _ les bril _ lan _ tes de joie _____ En des peaux jau _ nes

très expressif

com _ me des o _ ran _ ges; Je voudrais voir des vê _ te _

_ments de ve _ lours _ Et des ha _ bits à lon _ gues fran _ ges.

⑨ Grave et modéré

Je voudrais voir des ca _ lu _

rall.

Grave et modéré
(♩=72)

_mets   en_tre des bou_ches Tout en_tou_rées de bar_be blan_che;

Je   vou_drais   voir   d'âpres marchands aux re_gards

lou_   _ches,   Et des ca_dis,   et des vi_zirs Qui du seul mou_ve

ment de leur doigt qui se penche Accordent vie   ou mort au gré   de leur dé

21

sir.

Je voudrais voir la

Perse, et l'Inde, et puis la Chine,

Les mandarins ventrus sous les om-brel-les, Et les prin-ces-ses aux mains fi-nes, Et les let-

Allegro

_trés   qui se que_rel_lent Sur la   po_é_sie   et sur la beau_

té;   Je vou

12

_drais   m'at_tar_der   au   pa_lais en_chan_té   Et

Très lent (♩=40)
très expressif

comme un voy_a_geur é_tran_ger Contem_pler à loi_sir   des pa_y_sa_ges

peints Sur des é_tof_fes en des ca_dres de sa_pin

A_vec un person_nage au milieu d'un verger;

rall.

13 Modéré (♩=72)

Modéré (♩=72)

Je vou_drais voir des as_sas_sins sou_ri_

_ant Du bour_reau qui coupe un

cou d'in _ no _ cent   A _ vec son grand sa _ bre cour _

_ bé d'O _ ri _ ent.

14 Modéré

Je vou _ drais voir   des pau _ vres et des rei _ nes;

Je vou _ drais voir   des ro _ ses et du sang;

Je vou_drais voir mou_rir d'a_mour ou bien de haine.

15 Lent (♩.= 40)

En é-le-vant comme Sindbad ma vieille tasse a _ ra_be De temps en temps jusqu'à mes lè_vres

_Pour interrompre le conte a_vec art...

II
La Flûte enchantée

à Madame RENÉ DE SAINT-MARCEAUX

MAURICE RAVEL

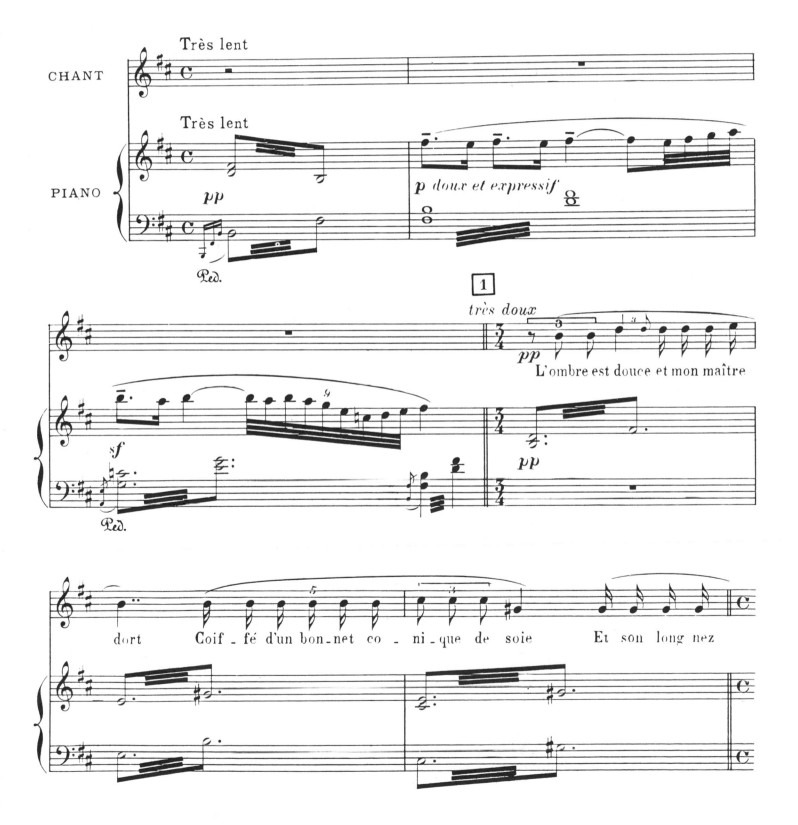

L'ombre est douce et mon maître dort Coif _ fé d'un bon-net co _ ni-que de soie Et son long nez

jaune en sa barbe blan _ che.

ad lib.

rapide

Allegro (♩=120) Mais moi, _____ je suis é_veil_lée en _ cor _____

Et j'é - coute au de - hors U - ne chan - son de

flûte où s'é - pan - che Tour à tour la tris - tesse ou la

joie.

-vo - le De la flû_te vers ma   joue Comme un mys_té_ri_eux bai -

rall.

ppp

5

- ser.

ppp

pp

rall.

I° Tempo

ppp

ppp

III
L'Indifférent

A Madame SIGISMOND BARDAC

MAURICE RAVEL

doux comme ceux d'u _ ne fil _ le, Jeune é _ tran _

_ ger, Et la cour_be fi _ ne De ton beau vi _ sa_ge de du_vet ombra_

_gé Est plus sé _ dui _ sante en _ cor de

li _ gne.

chan - te sur le pas de ma por - te U - ne langue in - con -

_nue et char _ man _ te ___ Comme u _ ne mu _ si _ que faus _ se.

En _ tre! Et que mon vin te ré _ con _ for _ te...

Mais non, tu pas _ ses Et de mon seuil je te vois t'é _ loi _ gner ___

au Mouv^t

Me fai_sant un dernier geste a_vec grâ _ ce Et la hanche lé_gè_re_ment ploy_

_ée Par ta dé_marche fé_mi_nine et las_se...

37

CINQ MÉLODIES POPULAIRES GRECQUES

Traduction française par
M.-D. CALVOCORESSI

acct de piano par
MAURICE RAVEL

I._ Chanson de la mariée

Ré _ veil _ le _ toi, ré_veil _ le toi, perdrix mi _

_gnon _ _ ne, Ah! Ré _ veil _ le _ toi, ré_veil _ le

38

toi, perdrix mi gnon _ _ _ ne. Ouvre au ma _

_tin tes ai _ _ _ _ _ les,

ouvre au ma _ tin tes ai _ _ _ _

_ les. Trois grains de beau _ té, mon

cœur en est brû _ lé! Trois grains de beau _

_ té, mon cœur en est brû _ lé.

Vois le ru _

_ ban, ie ru _ ban d'or que je t'ap _ por _ _ te.

Si tu veux, ma bel _ _ _le, viens nous ma _ _ ri _

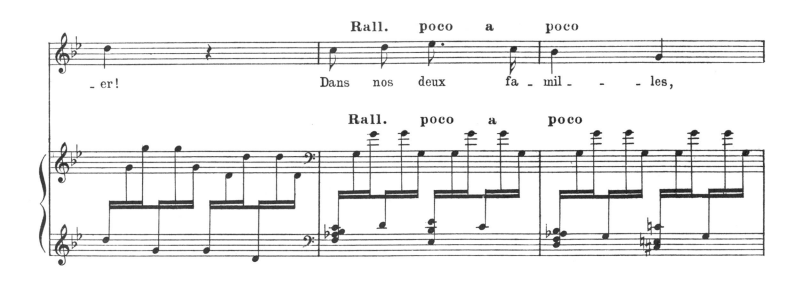

Rall. poco a poco

_ er! Dans nos deux fa _ mil _ _ _les,

tous sont al _ _ _li _ és!

II._ Là-bas, vers l'église

-glise Ay-io Costanndi- _ _no se sont ré-u-nis, _

ras-sem-blés en nombre in_fi _ ni, du monde, ô Vier-ge sain _ _

-te, du mon _ _ de tous les plus bra_ _ _ ves! _

pp

44

III._ Quel galant m'est comparable

Vois, pen _ _ dus, pen _ dus à ma cein _ tu _ _ re,

pis _ to_lets et sabre ai _ _ gu... Et c'est toi que

j'ai _ _ _ me!

IV._ Chanson des cueilleuses de lentisques

coeur___ toi que j'aime ar _ dem _ ment,___ tu es plus

beau, plus beau qu'un an _ ge.___

O _____ lors_que tu pa _ rais, an _ ge si

doux,_____ an _ ge si doux de_vant nos

48

yeux.

comme un bel an _ _ ge blond, sous le clair so _ _ leil,

Hé _ _ _ las! tous nos _____ pauvres cœurs sou _

_ pi _ _ _ rent!

V._ Tout gai!

Bel _ le jam _ _ be, ti _ re _ li, qui dan _ _ se;

Bel _ le jam _ _ be, la vais _ sel _ le dan _ se,_____

_____ Tra la la la la! la _ ra _ la, la

la, la la la la la, la _ ï la, la

la la la la la,   la la la la

la la la la la la la   la la la la

Rall.   a Tempo

la la la la laï la,   tra la la la la.

suivez

a Tempo

À Madame JEAN CRUPPI.

NOËL DES JOUETS.

MAURICE RAVEL.

Cou-vrent leurs ai - gres mir-li - tons.

pp innocemment

pp

pp

pp

p expressif

Vier-ge Ma - rie, en cri-no-li - ne, Ses yeux d'é - mail

p expressif

sans cesse ou - verts,____ En at-ten - dant Bonhomme hi -ver Veil-le Jé -

sus qui se do - di - ne

Car, près de là, sous un sa - pin, fur-tif, em-mi-touf - flé dans l'om-bre Du

bois Bel - zé - buth, le chien som - bre

Guet - te l'En - fant de su - cre peint

un peu plus vite qu'au début et en accélérant jusqu'au **ff**

cédez très peu

ppp

Ped.

Et leur vol de clin - quant ver - meil   Qui cli - quette en

ppp

bruits sy - mé - tri - ques   S'ac - corde au bé -

p   *cresc.* - - -

tail mé - ca - ni - que   Dont la voix

mf

mf

grê - le bê - - - - le: „No-

Allegro.

- ël! _____ No-ël! _____ No-ël! _____

Allegro.

Ped. jusqu'à la fin

HISTOIRES NATURELLES

Paroles de
JULES RENARD

à Madame JANE BATHORI

Musique de
MAURICE RAVEL
(1906)

I.-Le Paon

Sans hâte et noblement

PIANO

p

ff — mf

p solennel

Il va sûre_ment se mari_er au jour_

p

_d'hui.   Ce de_vait être pour hi_er.   En ha_bit de ga_

pp

mf

_la, il é_tait prêt. Il n'at_ten_dait que sa fiancée. Elle n'est pas ve_nue.

Elle ne peut tarder. Glo_

_rieux,_____ il se pro_mène a _ vec une al _ lure de prince in _ _

_dien et porte sur lui les riches pré_sents d'usage ___

L'a _ mour a _ _ _ vive l'é _ clat de ses cou _ leurs et

son aigrette tremble comme u _ ne lyre.

La fiancée n'arrive pas.

II

monte au haut du toit et re _ garde du cô _ té du so _ leil. _____

Il jette son cri dia_bo_lique:

Lé_on! ___ Lé_on! ___

C'est ain_si qu'il ap_pelle sa fiancée.

Il ne voit rien ve_

_nir   et personne ne ré_pond.

Les vo_lailles ha_bi_tuées ne lèvent même point la

tête.   Elles sont   lasses de l'admi _ rer.

Il re_des_

_cend dans la cour, si sûr d'être beau _____ qu'il est in_ca_pable de ran_cune.

Son mari_age se_ra pour de_main.

Et, ne sachant que faire du reste de la journée, il se di_rige vers le per_

_ron. Il gravit les marches, comme des marches de

tem _ ple, d'un pas of _ fi _ ciel.

Il re _ lè _ ve

sa robe à queue toute lourde des yeux qui n'ont pu se dé _ tacher d'elle.

Avec majesté

Rall.

Il ré _ pète en _ core une fois la

_ cé _ ré _ monie.

II.– Le Grillon

C'est l'heure _____ où, las d'er-
-rer, l'insec-te nè-gre revient de prome-nade et ré-pare a-vec soin le désordre
de son domaine.

D'a_bord il ra_tisse ses é _ troites allées de sable.

II

fait du bran de scie qu'il é _ carte au seuil de sa re _ traite.

Il lime la ra _ cine de cette grande herbe propre à le har_ce_ler.

Il se re_pose.

Puis il remonte sa minuscule mon _ tre.

A volonté

A-t-il fi _ ni? est-elle cas_sée? Il se re_pose encore un peu. Il ren_tre chez

suivez

lui et ferme sa porte.____ Longtemps il tourne sa clef dans la serrure dé_li_

_cate. Et il é _ coute: Point d'alarme de _ hors.

Mais il ne se trouve pas en sûreté.

Et comme par une chaînette

dont la poulie grince, il des_cend jusqu'au fond de la terre.

On n'entend plus rien.

Dans la campagne mu_

_ette, les peupliers se dressent comme des doigts en l'air et désignent la lu_ne.

III.. Le Cygne

69

_ages floconneux qu'il voit naître,   bouger,   et se per_dre dans l'eau.

C'est l'un d'eux qu'il dé _ si _ re.

Il le vi_se du bec,   et il plonge tout à coup   son col vê_tu de

nei _ ge.   Puis,   tel un bras de femme sort d'une

manche, il le re _ tire. Il n'a rien.

en se perdant

Il regarde : les nu _ ages ef_fa_rouchés ont dis_pa_ru.

Plus lent qu'au début

Il ne reste qu'un instant dé_sa_bu _ sé, car les nu_a_ges tardent peu à reve_

_nir, et, là - bas, où meurent les on_du_lations de l'eau,

71

en voi_ci un   qui se reforme.

Reprenez   le   1ᵉʳ Mouvᵗ   Dou_ce_ment,

sur son lé_ger cous_sin de plumes,_____   le cy_gne rame   et s'ap_

proche...   Il s'é

72

Ralentissez

puise ____ à pêcher de vains reflets, et peut-être qu'il mourra, victime de cette il_lu_sion,

Ralentissez

Très lent   **Ralentissez**

a_vant d'attra-per un seul morceau de nu_age. ____

Très lent   **Ralentissez**

pp très expressif   *ppp*

Modéré   *mp*   *p*

Mais qu'est-ce que je dis ?   Chaque fois qu'il plonge, il fouil_le du bec la

Modéré

pp   *p très sec et bien rythmé*

vase nourrissante ____ et ramène un ver.   Il engraisse comme une oie.

Sans ralentir

mp

pp

73

IV.– Le Martin-Pêcheur

On ne peut plus lent

CHANT

PIANO

Ça n'a pas mor_du, ce soir, mais je rap-

_porte une rare émotion. Comme je tenais ma perche de ligne ten_due, un martin-pêcheur est ve-

_nu s'y poser. Nous n'avons pas d'oiseau plus é_cla_tant

Très calme

Il semblait une grosse fleur bleue au bout d'une longue tige. La perche pliait sous le poids.

Je ne res_pi_rais plus, tout

fier d'être pris pour un arbre par un mar_tin-pê_cheur.

Et je suis sûr qu'il ne s'est pas envo_ lé de peur,   mais qu'il a

cru qu'il ne fai_sait que pas _ ser d'une   branche à une autre.

à ROGER DUCASSE

V. _ La Pintade

_pite   et les har _ cèle.

Retenez beaucoup   *court*

au Mouv^t

Puis elle baisse sa tête,   penche le corps,

et, de toute la vi_tesse de ses pattes maigres,   elle court   frapper, de son bec

dur,   juste au centre de la roue d'u_ne dinde.

glissando

Cette po-seuse l'agaçait.

Ain _ _ si,   la tê _ te bleui_e,   ses barbil_lons à   vif,

co_car_dière,___ el_le ra _ ge du ma_tin au soir.

Elle   se   bat sans mo_^tif,   peut - être

parce qu'elle s'i_ma_gine toujours qu'on se moque de sa taille, de son crâ_ne chauve

et de sa queue basse. Et elle ne cesse de je_ter un cri discor_

_dant qui per_ce l'air comme une pointe.

Parfois elle quitte la cour et dispa_

rait. Elle laisse aux vo_lailles pa_ci_fiques un mo_ment de ré_

pit.

Mais el_le re_vient plus tur_bu_lente et plus cri_

_ar__de. Et,____ fré_né_tique, elle se vautre par

terre.

Qu'a-t-elle donc ? La sournoise fait une farce.

Elle est allée pondre son œuf à la cam_pagne. Je peux le chercher si ça m'amuse.

Et elle se roule dans la pous_sière _____ comme une bos_sue.

81

VOCALISE-ÉTUDE

(EN FORME DE HABANERA)

Maurice RAVEL

LES GRANDS VENTS VENUS D'OUTREMER...

Poésie de
HENRI DE RÉGNIER

Musique de
MAURICE RAVEL
(1906)

PIANO

Les grands vents ve_nus d'outre -

- mer Pas _ sent par la vil _ le, l'hi _ ver,

Com _ me des

Original key: E-flat minor.

é _ tran _ gers a _ mers.

en dehors

calme

Ils se con _ cer _ tent, gra _ ves et pâ _ les, Sur les

Très lent
calme

m.d.

pp

m.g.

1 Corde

pla _ ces, et leurs san _ da _ les En _ sa _ blent le

mf

p

m.d.

mf

p

m.g.

3 Cordes

qui l'hor _ loge est mor _ _ _ _ te.

Retenez

à volonté

Et les a _ do _ les _ cents a _ mers   S'en vont a _ vec eux vers la mer. ___

Lent
très lointain

SUR L'HERBE

Poésie de
PAUL VERLAINE

Musique de
MAURICE RAVEL
(1907)

Moins, Ca_margo, que vo_tre nu_que.

au Mouvᵗ

Ma flam _ _me... Do, mi, sol, la, si.

_L'ab_bé, ta noir_ceur se dé_voi_le.

Retenez

CHANSON ESPAGNOLE

CHANT POPULAIRE

Primée au 5ᵉ concours de la *Maison du Lied* de Moscou (1910)

Traduction française
de la *Maison du Lied*

Harmonisation de
MAURICE RAVEL

94

CHANSON FRANÇAISE

CHANT POPULAIRE

LIMOUSIN

Primée au 5ᵉ concours de la *Maison du Lied* de Moscou (1910)

Harmonisation de
MAURICE RAVEL

Jean_ne_ton où i_rons-nous___ gar___ der, Jean_ne_ton où i_rons-nous___ gar___ der
Ja _ ne _ ta ount a _ ni _ rem___ gar _ dar, Ja _ ne _ ta ount a _ ni _ rem___ gar _ dar

Qu'a _ yons bon une heu_re? Lan la! Qu'a _ yons bon une heu _ _ re?
Qu'a_jam boun tems un' ou _ ra? Lan la! Qu'a_jam boun tems un' ou _ _ ra?

a Tempo

Là - bas, là - bas,___ au pré___ bar . ré Là - bas, là - bas,___ au pré___ bar . ré,
A - val, a - val,___ al prat___ bar . rat; A - val, a - val,___ al prat___ bar . rat,

a Tempo

Y'a de tant bel . les ombres Lan la! Y'a de tant bel . les om . bres.
Ia de tan be . las oumbras! Lan la! Ia de tan be . las oum . bras.

Ri - te - nu - to

Ri - te - nu - to

a Tempo

Jean _ nette a tel _ le _ ment__ jou _ é,   Jean _ nette a tel _ le _ ment__ jou _ é

Ja _ ne _ ta a ta _ la _ men__ jou _ gat,   Ja _ ne _ ta a ta _ la _ men__ jou _ gat

a Tempo

Que s'y est ou _ bli _ é _ e, Lan la!   Que s'y est ou _ bli _ é _ _ e!

Que se ies ou _ bli _ da _ da, Lan la!   Que se ies ou _ bli _ da _ _ da!

Ral _ len _ tan _ do

CHANSON ITALIENNE

ROMAINE

CHANT POPULAIRE

Primée au 5ᵉ concours de la *Maison du Lied* de Moscou (1910)

Traduction française
de la *Maison du Lied*

Harmonisation de
MAURICE RAVEL

Je cla _ me mon a _ mour, _____ nul qui ré _
Chia _ mo l'a _ mo _ re mio, _____ nun m'ar _ ris _

_pon _ de _____ Je cla _ me mon a _
_pon _ de _____ Chia _ _ mo l'a _ mo _ re

_ mour, _____ nul qui ré _ pon _ de! _____
mio, _____ nun m'ar _ ris _ pon _ de. _____

CHANSON HÉBRAÏQUE

Primée au 5ᵉ concours de la *Maison du Lied* de Moscou (1910)

Traduction française
de la *Maison du Lied*

Harmonisation de
MAURICE RAVEL

vit chante gloire au Sei _ _ _ gneur, pè _ re mien. Ce qui vit chante gloire au Sei _ _ _ gneur,
chai _____ joi _ du _ _ cho," Ta _ tu _ nju. "Kol chai _____ joi _ du _ _ cho,"

Tempo I⁰

pè _ _ re mien. Ma _ yer _ ke, mon fils,
Ta _ _ tu _ nju. Me _ jer _ ke, main Suhn,

Ma _ yer _ ke, mon fils, ô Ma _ yer _ ke, mon fils, Mais tu veux en _ co _ re du pain? Mais
Me _ jer _ ke, main Suhn, oi Me _ jer _ ke, main Suhn, Oif wo _ darfs tu M'su _ nei? Oif

108

Trois Poèmes de Stéphane Mallarmé

I. – Soupir

à IGOR STRAWINSKY

tom _ _ ne jon _ ché   de   ta _ ches de rous _ seur

Et   vers le ciel er _ rant   de ton œil an _ gé _ li _ _ _

_ _ que   Mon _ _ te,   com _ me dans un jar _ din mé _ lan _ co _

-li _ _ _ que, Fi _ dè _ _ _ _ _ le, un blanc jet

Ped. jusqu' à

d'eau sou _ pi _ re vers l'A _ zur!

112

Vers l'A_zur at_ten_dri d'Oc_to_bre pâle et pur_____ Qui

mire aux grands bassins sa lan_gueur in_fi_nie_____

Un peu plus lent

Et lais_se,_____ sur l'eau morte où la

1er Mouvt

113

fauve a _ go _ nie Des feuil _ les erre au vent_____ et creuse un froid sil _ lon,_____

Se traî _ ner le so _ leil jau _ ne d'un long ray _

_ on.

Clarens, 2 Avril, 1413

114

II. _ Placet futile

à FLORENT SCHMITT

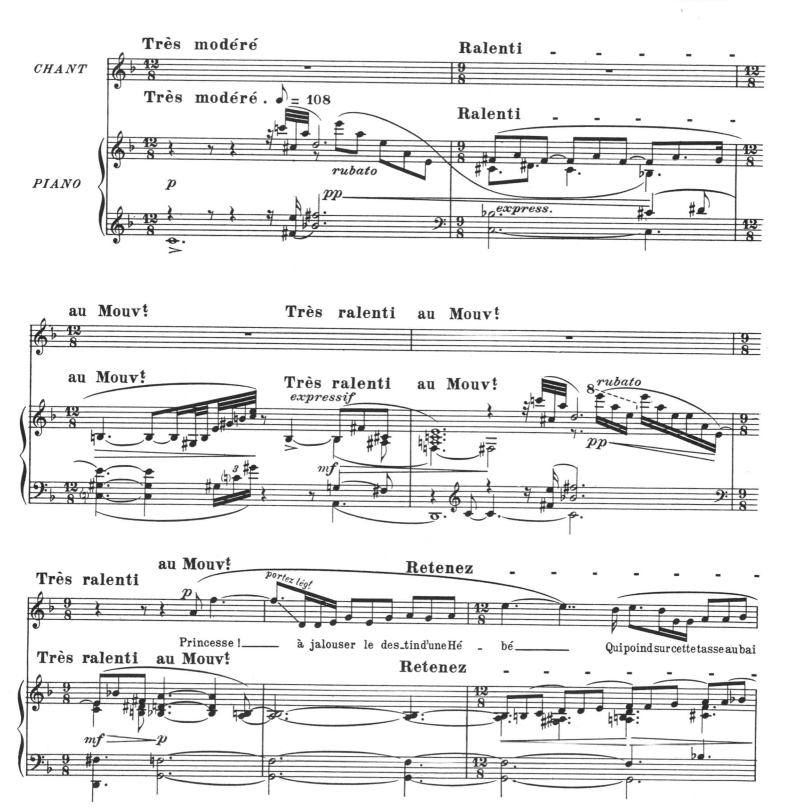

Princesse !_____ à jalouser le des_tind'une Hé _ bé_____ Qui poind sur cette tasse au bai

Un peu plus lent

_ser de vos lè _ _ vres   J'u_se mes feux   mais n'ai rang discret que d'abbé_

De plus en plus lent

— Et ne fi_gu_re_rai mê_me nu sur le Sè _ vres_

Modérément animé ♪ = 132

Ossia

Modérément animé

116

Com__me je ne suis pas ton bi __ chon em __ bar __ bé,____

expressif

expressif

Ralentissez __ __ **peu** __ __ **à** __ __ **peu** __ __

__ Ni la pas_til __ le, ni du rou __ ge, ni jeux mie __ __ vres

Ralentissez __ __ **peu** __ __ **à** __ __ **peu**

pp

p

pp

pp

p

III.– Surgi de la croupe et du bond

à *ERIK SATIE*

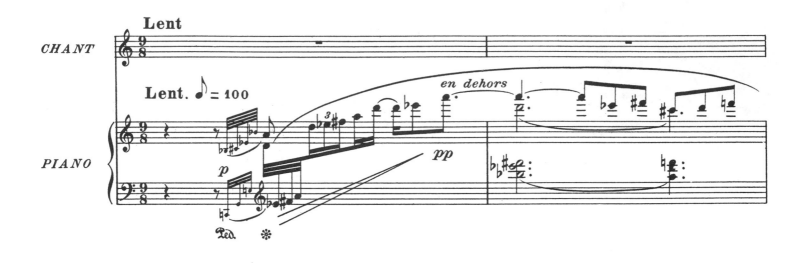

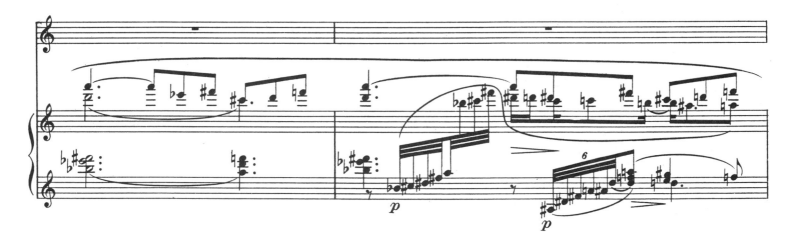

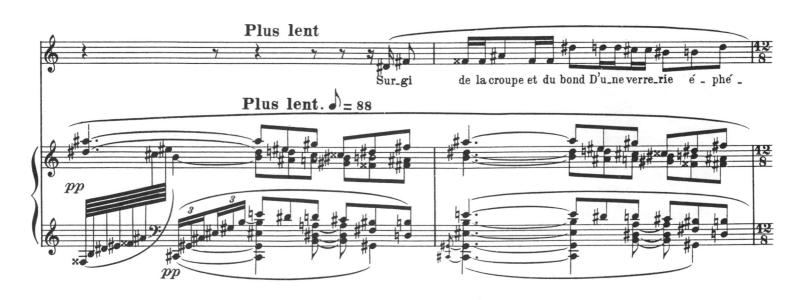

_mè_ re Sans fleurir la veillée amè _ re _____ Le col ignoré s'interrompt.

Je crois bien que deux bouches n'ont Bu, ni son a _ mant ni ma mè _ re

_____ Jamais à la même chimè _ re Moi, sylphe de ce froid pla _ fond! _____

Le pur va _ se d'aucun breuva _ ge Que l'i _ nexhaus _ ti_ble veu_va _ ge_____ A _ go _

St Jean-de-Luz
Août 1913.

122

DEUX MÉLODIES HÉBRAÏQUES

I. Kaddisch

MAURICE RAVEL

vey _ am _ _ _ li'kh mal' _ khou _ _ té   be _
et res _ su _ ci _ ter les tré _ pas _ sés   Ton

hay _ _ _ _ _ _ _ _ yé'khòn, ou _ ve _ yo _ me'khôn ou _ ve'hay _
rè _ _ _ _ _ _ _ _ gne, A _ do _ na _ ï, soit pro_cla_

_ yé _____ de'khol beth yis_ra _ ël___ ba _ 'a _
_ mé _____ par nous, fils d'Is_ra _ ël, ___ au _ jour _

124

II. L'Enigme Eternelle

MAURICE RAVEL

Ent - fernt men
L'on ré - pond:
Tra la la la la la
Tra la la la la la

la la la
la la la
Tra la la la
Tra la la la la
Un as
Si l'on

men will ken - nen sa - gen
ne peut te ré - pon - dre:
Tra la la la tra la la la
Tra la la la tra la la la

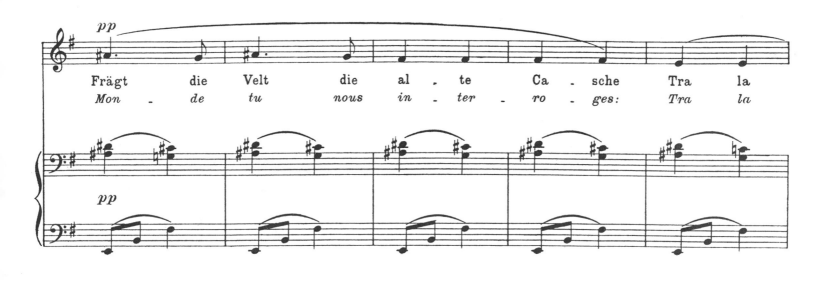

Frägt die Velt die al_te Ca_sche Tra la

Mon _ de tu nous in _ ter _ ro _ ges: Tra la

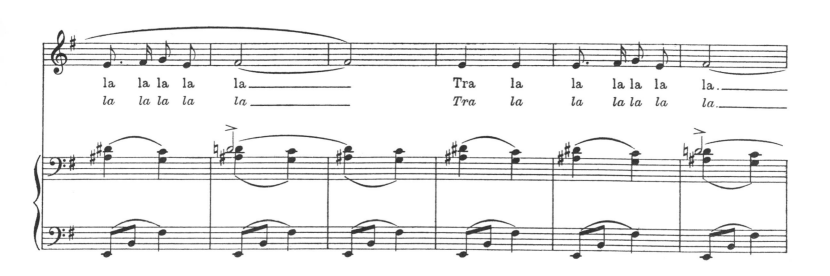

la la la la la_____ Tra la la la la la la._____

la la la la la_____ Tra la la la la la la._____

perdendo

Ped

Mai 1914